Longer

No Longer

I

The Power Of the Gospel
Like You Have Never Heard It Before

JACOB HOTCHKISS

NO LONGER I

First Edition 2020

ISBN: 9798582003106

Published by Happy Self Publishing
www.happyselfpublishing.com

TABLE OF CONTENTS

INTRODUCTION

I have become deeply convicted in recent days that there is another great step for the Church to take in our understanding of the gospel. I do not mean anything new (though perhaps new to many of us), but greater comprehension of that which was written across the pages of Scripture thousands of years ago. Among those who look to Jesus Christ as their Lord and Savior, there are disturbingly few who understand how the finished work of Christ actually brings about its intended effect — sanctification. Humbly, I suggest that it may not matter whether you have heard the gospel a thousand times, been in church your whole life, read volumes of Christian literature, or spent years in ministry and a good seminary. I fit all those categories, and while they provided somewhat of a foundation for my own spiritual life and ministry, there was a piece of that foundation that was always missing, a crack right down the middle that left it weak and unstable.

I am confident that this has little or nothing to do with the specific tradition I come from or the particular books that I have read (or have not read). For I have yet to find any stream of the Christian faith or any literature whatsoever (besides the Bible) that teaches these things well. I assume that they are out there; I just do not know where. Yet I believe that it should be widespread knowledge in the

Church. And more, I feel that nearly all of my Christian brothers and sisters, regardless of our typical variances in beliefs, can find common ground here. It is Solid Rock, and it is time we learn to build upon it.

I tell you truly, what God has accomplished for those who trust in the name of Jesus is so immeasurably great and inconceivably marvelous that to comprehend and believe it *entirely* would instantaneously render any person unrecognizable, brightly shining with the glory of God. This sort of profound life-transformation is not a unique grace given to a select, lucky few (like the Apostle Paul, for instance). Nor is it a gift given only to the "holy elite" who have unusual amounts of passion and time for the things of God. It is for every person who believes. There should be no question that the message of Christianity promises anything less.

This being the case, we must ask what is missing in the Church, perhaps even in our own lives. If our gospel is actually this powerful, how have we so failed to realize its promises? Why is it that we are not further along this path to sanctification? How does sin still have such a hold on God's people? We know, in theory, that we are to become like Christ and that "with God, all things are possible" (Matthew 19:26). But in practice, this has been more difficult than it ought to be. Whether it be in our personal struggles with sin or our ministry to others who need freedom, I believe most would say that they have seen and experienced relatively unimpressive results (besides the occasional exception) compared to what we read about in the Bible. Thus, in frustration, disappointment, or whatever it may be, we have settled for a gospel that is not quite as wonderful as the one we originally hoped to be true.

We need not blame anyone, and there is certainly no fruit to bear from pointing fingers, anyway. For the sake of our discussion, let us attribute the current state of things to the simple fact that we cannot know what we have not heard. "And how are they to hear without someone preaching?" (Romans 10:14) It may be especially difficult for those who have been in Christian leadership or scholarship to admit that we have missed anything so important, but I implore the Church to keep pride out of the picture. What matters most is the salvation of souls, including our own. And if, in fact, what I say is true (which is still for you to determine), then the next great move of God will almost certainly include the dissemination of this knowledge to his Church. It is that important. It is that powerful. And you will not want to miss it. There is little doubt in my mind that if the Church can broadly comprehend and embrace the good news in its original, apostolic form, the sheer magnitude of revival (personal and corporate) will be like nothing we have ever seen before.

The gospel should always have this kind of effect, and it is an effect that does not wear off. Once we see it clearly, we do not become numb to it, but evermore aware of it. We do not grow tired of it but are increasingly energized by it. We do not feel the need to move on to other things, but to see it more sharply. It is an entirely sufficient foundation for the day-to-day life of every Christian, a never-ending fuel for the fire that is within us.

Jesus said, "the truth will set you free" (John 8:32). So tell me, Christian, does your understanding of the truth explain how the truth *itself* is the mechanism for change? Does your understanding of the gospel explain how belief *alone*, when it is present and active, makes sin impossible and righteousness inevitable? Does your knowledge of God's grace propel you daily out of your old ways and into the new, like a cannonball shot out of a cannon? Has it proven to be enough in every moment to keep you living above your feelings and your circumstances, bearing the fruit of the Spirit, always rejoicing and giving thanks for the hope that is within you? And just as importantly, does it have the same effect on those with whom you share it? If not, it is very likely that you do not have the whole picture, or otherwise, you have simply forgotten it. In this case, my sincere hope is to bring a greater level of clarity and conviction into your life regarding the gospel in which you believe.

For a very long time now, God has been working to restore the Church to its original understanding of the gospel as it is plainly written in Scripture. Some will be inclined to think there is no need for this, as if we already have it. They may feel it is off-putting to even suggest such a thing. "Who are you to think you have a deeper understanding of the gospel?" they will say. And the truth is, I am no one — just a believer doing his best to share what God has shared with me through Scripture, through other Christians, and through his Holy Spirit who guides us into all truth (see John 16:13). I do not personally claim to have the fullest picture of it. I simply intend to move the needle a little bit further, hoping that others will take it all the way. Whether or not I get everything exactly right is actually not my greatest concern. I am far from infallible and remain open to correction. Yet still, I am compelled by God to share what I believe with the same level of conviction that I believe it. It is up to you to discern for yourself what is true.

One of the most common concerns I hear when I begin to speak of the gospel as I do in this book is, "If this is true, then why have I never heard it before?" Or, "If this is true, then why hasn't God revealed it to his church up to this point?" I do not pretend to know the answer to that question, but I do know where you can find it. Look back five hundred years to the Protestant Reformation. If you can tell me how the gospel became so perverted that the selling of indulgences for the forgiveness of sins was common practice in the Church for roughly five hundred years, then you will have your answer. How is it that the most basic essence of the gospel — salvation by grace through faith in Jesus Christ — was almost entirely lost to the Church until then? I have no idea. It is downright baffling. But it happened.

Hindsight is 20/20, but let us not be blind to the moment we are in. It is much easier to recognize the changes that needed to happen in the past than to recognize our own current lack of understanding and need for theological reformation. It would be just as foolish to think we see it all clearly today as it would be to think that the Church saw things clearly then. It should not offend us one bit that God has more work to do in this regard. If we desire to bear fruit, we should always be eager for more of God's truth.

A FEW POINTS OF CLARITY

1. It is important to state that *sanctification* is the primary matter at hand. You might call this something different — like spiritual growth, maturity, holiness, imparted righteousness, the character of God, perfecting love, the fruit of the Spirit, overcoming sin, etc. — any of which is fine, as long as we can agree, without exception, that

it is an important result of the Christian life. As we follow Jesus, we should look more and more like him. If you do not agree with this statement, you might as well stop reading now and pick up your Bible. Our conversation will be fruitless, and God's grace to you highly limited until you learn of this truth and embrace it.

2. We need not agree at this point about the details of sanctification — what exactly it looks like, how quickly it occurs, or the degree to which it is possible in this life. All these are secondary and unnecessary squabbles compared to the issue at hand, which is *how God brings about the fruit of sanctification in our lives through the finished work of Jesus Christ.* Part of God's good news is that Jesus transforms us, and we want to know how to receive this gift in the fullest way possible. This is our focus, and it is a big deal. Let us not get caught straining out gnats while swallowing a camel (see Matthew 23:24).

3. The ways that the Church most commonly understands the gospel today are not so much false as they are incomplete. By themselves, they fail to capture the fullest essence of the gospel, which makes the most complete use of our faith and God's grace. Moreover, I think you will find that much of what has been missing in the Church is the *practical application* of the gospel in our daily lives so that we may walk in truth and realize its intended effect — freedom. Once you see it, you cannot unsee it. It will shape and inform every area of your life and ministry moving forward.

TIPS FOR READING THIS BOOK

1. A heads up: The first and second chapters are, admittedly, a little denser than the others, yet I felt they were a necessary theological foundation for the rest. If you find yourself getting a little bogged down here, don't give up. One of my editors described these chapters as the slow upward climb of a roller coaster, whereas chapter three and onward are like the downward free fall — easy and fast. If you are like me and are especially excited about the chapters that focus on practical application, that begins in Chapter 7. I tell you this so that, if you cannot wait, you may decide to skip there and then come back around to the theological foundation that I set up in the first six chapters. Both are very important.

2. I highly encourage the reader, each time that I reference the Bible, to stop and think about how it is that the Bible passage makes the point that I am trying to make. My most common reason for referencing Scripture is not to prove my point, rather, it is to show the reader what the Scripture means (or at least what I believe it to mean). The points that I will be making are intended to serve the Scripture, not the other way around. The majority of this book, for that matter, is intended to help the reader better understand the gospel within the pages of their Bible. Therefore, when I am building a case for something, please do not simply take my word for it. Open your own Bible, humble yourself before God, pray that he will help you to understand, and believe that in time, he will. In this way, I hope that you will have no need to reference this

book after reading it as Scripture itself will have become your reference guide for truth.

3. In this process, I believe that it matters a great deal which Bible translation you use. Given the specific content we will be covering in this book, the more literal the translation, the better. At the very least, it is important that your Bible tells you in a footnote when it has chosen to use a different word or wording than what is found in the original language. For this book, I have chosen the English Standard Version for all my Bible references. This is for two basic reasons. One, I am personally very familiar with it. Two, its relatively close adherence to the original language makes it plenty suitable for the task at hand.

4. It is God's desire for you to understand spiritual things, most notably his gospel. But I am utterly convinced — and Scripture says as much — that no one can obtain knowledge of the things of God through their own intellect (see 1 Corinthians 2:10-16). The transfer of knowledge is good and necessary, or else there would be no reason for me to write this book. But knowledge will never bear lasting fruit if it does not become *revelation* within the heart. We do not need to be scared by the word "revelation." We are not seeking to come up with anything new, rather, we are seeking to understand personally and deeply what God has already revealed about himself. He is happy and ready to do this for *every* humble believer who asks. *Knowledge becomes revelation through prayer.* So as you read, I implore you also to pray.

The gospel is not for those who think of themselves as wise. We must believe that it can be understood by anyone with the Spirit of God. The Church does not need more intellectual giants. It needs more spiritual giants. And we should never confuse the former with the latter. Let us put to death our fascination and reliance on man's intellect. And let us put on the mind of Christ, relying fully on him to understand his word.

"I do not cease to give thanks for you, remembering you in my prayers, that the God of our Lord Jesus Christ, the Father of glory, may give you the Spirit of wisdom and of revelation in the knowledge of him, having the eyes of your hearts enlightened, that you may know what is the hope to which he has called you, what are the riches of his glorious inheritance in the saints, and what is the immeasurable greatness of his power toward us who believe, according to the working of his great might..." (Ephesians 1:16–19)

Chapter 1

THE SUBTLER FORM OF WORKS-RIGHTEOUSNESS

"For I do not understand my own actions. For I do not do what I want, but I do the very thing I hate" (Romans 7:15).

There is no way to know for sure, but this might be the most relatable verse in all the Bible. In one sentence, Paul sums up what is one of the greatest conundrums of our human existence. Why do we sin, even when we desire not to? Christian or not, if there is any good in you at all, you know what it is like to "have the desire to do what is right, but not the ability to carry it out" (Romans 7:18). Maybe you are a parent who wants to be more gentle and loving with your kids, but you find yourself almost incapable of going a day without an outburst of anger. Or maybe you are a spouse who wants to be more present and thoughtful, but the pressures of work or the cares of life always get the best of your attention. Maybe you genuinely want to forgive and move on, but within you is a bitterness that is seemingly too sweet to leave behind. We all have planned to be done with that "thing" — overeating, substance abuse, pornography, laziness, negativity, you name it — only to find ourselves doing it again within days or weeks. When will we finally be done? We know that social media breeds jealousy and insecurity; the news breeds fear and anxiety. They make us feel awful, but we feel even worse when we are not following them. So we mindlessly scroll. We *know*, beyond a shadow of a doubt, that money can't buy happiness. The very reason this phrase is so cliché is because it is so profoundly and obviously true. Yet we live as if money can buy happiness, going on about life miserably obsessed with financial freedom and material comfort. I could keep going, but you get the point.

To a great degree, we intuitively know better than to give ourselves to these things which do not benefit the soul and have little or no eternal value. But we cannot help ourselves. Deep down, even though we despise these things, there is a part of us that apparently loves them, too. The plethora of secular content today that is devoted to the area of self-help is evidence of the fact that we genuinely desire to be our "best" selves (whatever that means), but also that there is something within us that makes this terribly difficult.

Desire to be better, or lack thereof, is not the problem in the way that some suppose. Nor is self-discipline the solution. We may have the noblest intentions, but at the end of the day, we remain slaves of instinct and passion. Simply put, the flesh is a beast of nature that no one can tame. We may overcome it in part, but we are never entirely free from this ongoing conflict within ourselves. Some appear to be doing better than others, sure. But when it comes to the hidden life — that which at every hour demands love, patience, joy, sacrifice, humility, mercy, self-control, etc. — it appears that no one comes close to any standard of perfection.[1] It seems the best remedy we have, then, is to give in, give up, or just give it our best. This is the kind of cheap, wholesale advice that our society (and even our Church) buys in bulk. To be fair, though, it is the only sane and comforting conclusion for those who recognize that they are in a lifelong war they cannot win.

This is where I found myself for many years as a Christian — desperately wanting to live a life pleasing to God but painfully aware of my inability to do so. The more I wanted it, the more it hurt, so it was usually easier to care a little bit less than I knew I should. Few passages in scripture brought me more comfort than Paul's words in the latter half of Romans 7. In some of the hardest times, I would cry out with him: "Wretched man that I am! Who will deliver me from this body of death? Thanks be to God through Jesus Christ our Lord!" (Romans 7:24-25) It was very comforting to know that even the mighty Apostle Paul felt like I did at times. It reminded me that there was nothing I could really do about all this, but the struggle was just part of the Christian life. We fight against sin; sin fights against us. We have some good days and some bad days; some wins

---

[1] You might wonder why I would even use such a word as "perfection" since it is so clear that no human being is perfect. But part of the Christian message is that Jesus Christ was a perfect human — sinless in thought, word, and deed — and he is the image to which we are being conformed (see Romans 8:29). Yes, we are to be as he is. If anyone has a contention on this point, it is not with me, but with Jesus. He himself said, "You therefore must be perfect, as your heavenly Father is perfect" (Matthew 5:48), after equating anger to murder, lust to adultery, and commanding us to love everyone, including our own enemies.

and some losses. It is difficult, but it is worth it. It will all be over someday when Jesus comes to deliver us.

There is just one problem. This is not the gospel! Nor is it an accurate interpretation of Paul's monologue (more on that in the next chapter). It may provide temporary relief, but is relief all that we desire? No. We want deliverance; we want victory; and we want it *now*, not in our distant future. Otherwise, it is hard to see in what way the gospel is any more helpful in our *day-to-day life* than the next best self-help book, or better, a few glasses of wine. But the gospel of Jesus Christ doesn't just shift the momentum; it changes the game entirely in a way that nothing else can. If our understanding of the gospel fails to explain how this is so, then believers will have little, if any, advantage in this life over non-believers, let alone any message worth sharing. This, I believe, is the sad case for much of the Church today, and it is time for that to change.

But before we go any further, let me be clear that this is not a self-help gospel. In fact, it could not be further from it — and thank God — for we have already determined that we cannot help ourselves. Moreover, this is not the way for you to become all that you *want* to be (unless, of course, you want to be holy). Rather, it is the way for you to become all that you were *created* to be. It is death to sin and life to God and nothing in between. It is full restoration, with no limit and no compromise. It is amazingly practical and wildly inconceivable. It is "the mystery hidden for ages and generations but now revealed to his saints" (Colossians 1:26). It is perfect freedom *today* for all who repent and believe.

THE POWER OF SIN IS THE LAW

Let us begin by reading Romans 7 all the way through. This passage will equip us with some great insight and serve as a solid foundation once we understand it properly. It may be helpful to leave your Bible open to this passage through this chapter and the next since we reference it and the surrounding scriptures quite frequently.

If you were to look for a theme in this chapter, you would probably notice the frequent use and connection between the ideas of *the law* and *sin*. From the outset, it is apparent that Paul wants his readers to know they have been released from the law through Christ. Why? Because despite the law's most obvious purpose which is to direct us toward obedience, being under the law actually undermines this goal, making it *more* difficult to obey God and enslaving us to sin.[2]

This, of course, was offensive to those first-century Jewish-Christians who held God and his law in high regard. To be clear, this "law" to which he refers may be understood, in its most general sense, as God's commands. So it seemed to them that Paul was denying the goodness and relevance of God's commands, although he was not. In reality, Paul was just acknowledging that we are like

---

[2] The argument goes like this. According to Paul, "the law came in to increase the [sin]" (Romans 5:20), "in order that sin might be shown to be sin, and through the commandment might become sinful beyond measure" (Romans 7:13). Thus, "[t]he very commandment that promised life proved to be death to me. For sin, seizing an opportunity through the commandment, deceived me and through it killed me" (Romans 7:10-11). In other words, although the law provided the rubric for righteousness, these rules only gave sin a name and an opportunity. "For I would not have known what it is to covet if the law had not said, "You shall not covet"" (Romans 7:7). In showing us how *not* to sin, the law also shows us how *to* sin. Thus, the passions of our flesh are "aroused by the law" (Romans 7:6).

children who do exactly what their parents tell them *not* to do. It is not the parents' fault for giving the right command, nor does it mean that the command should not have been given. For "the commandment is holy and righteous and good" (Romans 7:12). Nonetheless, it is through the command that we are tempted to sin.

This is why Paul taught that "the power of sin is the law" (1 Corinthians 15:56, cf. Romans 6:14). *Despite* the goodness of God's commands, to be "under" them is to be under the control of sin. But to be free from the law is to be free from sin, "in order that we may bear fruit for God" (Romans 7:4).

This being the case, it is of the utmost importance that we Christians live as ones who are *truly* no longer under the law. Otherwise, sin will control us. Yet, at the same time, we cannot completely do away with the law as if God's commandments are not relevant to us anymore. They certainly are (see Romans 3:31). Hence, one of the great enigmas in Christianity. How can we take holiness seriously without becoming once again enslaved to the law? How can we live completely under grace without the risk of becoming entitled or irresponsible with that grace? How can we insist on obedience to God's commands while also insisting that obedience is no longer a means to salvation? How can we preach that it is "all by grace through faith" without diminishing the costly nature of discipleship? Etc.

Many have wrestled with this seeming contradiction, and like me, they have felt either misunderstood, stupid, or crazy, despite the fact that their intuition is correct — the gospel has to be better than this. In our Church today, it seems there are essentially two options: (1) Try harder. (2) Stop trying so hard. The former leads to legalism, and the latter to licentiousness³. Both leave the Christian in the grips of sin. Luckily for us, this problem is not new, and the solution is written across the pages of Scripture.

THE OBEDIENCE OF FAITH

If we take an even broader scope of Romans, we find a predominant theme throughout the whole letter. In the first and last paragraphs of Romans, Paul states that it is his apostolic duty "to bring about the *obedience of faith*" (Romans 1:5, 16:26; my italics). This provides some good context for the letter. Paul is on a quest to explain how believers are made righteous — that is, without sin — by faith alone, as opposed to the usual means of striving.

> "For by works of the law no human being will be justified [made righteous] in his sight, since through the law comes knowledge of sin... But now the righteousness of God has been manifested apart from the law... the righteousness of God through faith in Jesus Christ for all who believe..." (Romans 3:20-22)

There is a very important word in this passage that reveals its meaning — *manifested*. When something is manifested, it is revealed, made known, brought into the light, etc. Notice, then, what is being manifested — *God's own* righteousness; and how it is manifested — by making *his people* righteous (i.e. justified) like him. Paul is writing

---

³ Here, I use "licentiousness" for its archaic meaning, which means basically an utter disregard for rules. It comes from the Latin word *licentia*, which means "freedom," and there is hardly a better word to describe the kind of abuse of one's newfound freedom in Christ that the Bible often warns against. (e.g. Galatians 5:13)

here about how God's perfect character, or moral uprightness, is made known to the world. And while God has always used his people for this task — we were made in his image, after all — he now brings about obedience in his people through their faith in Jesus Christ, rather than their subjugation to the law.

Therefore, faith and grace are never contrary to obedience as if they give us a license to sin. Rather, in the Christian life, they are the very *means* to obedience. Our faith in God's grace is actually the *only* thing that delivers us from sin, whereas our sheer will to obey God's law — no matter how determined we are — is never enough. "[F]or all have sinned and fall short of the glory of God" (Romans 3:23)

It would be difficult to overstate the importance of this point. Since the earliest days of the Church, Christians have struggled with the practical implications of faith and grace. The natural mind intuitively feels like a call to holiness is something that must be added to the gospel of grace to "balance" the message. Otherwise, we might just go on sinning. The natural mind thinks that *in addition* to believing the gospel, we must *then* obey God — as if you can do one without the other. The result is that well-meaning Christians (myself included), using their natural minds, have tainted the gospel by adding works of the law back into it, unintentionally subjecting one another to slavery once again.

Paul preached a radical message — where we are released from law and need only to believe — and he was constantly being accused of promoting a gospel where obedience is optional, and sin is encouraged (see Romans 3:8). This is the context for questions like these: "Are we to sin that grace may abound?" (Romans 6:1) Or, "Are we to sin because we are not under law but under grace?" (Romans 6:15) The intended readers were not looking for an excuse to sin. Rather, they had a great appreciation for the law and desired to obey God (see Romans 6:17). But that is exactly where the issue arises. They could not see how a person was accountable to obey God if the person was "not under law but under grace" (Romans 6:14) as Paul said they were. They could not see how obedience was relevant in the context of grace. It seemed to them that Paul's message of "grace alone through faith alone" was an *excuse* to sin, whereas only God's law gave the believer a responsibility to obey. Thus, they wondered, how could God do away with works of the law *entirely*?

But as we just mentioned, it was Paul's point to prove that faith in God's grace is never an excuse to sin. It is the very way that a person is freed from sin. Failure to understand this is what kept these early Christians hanging onto the law as the daily means to holiness, and, to their surprise, what kept them in captivity to sin. I suggest to you here that the Church has been doing this — just a little more subtly and unknowingly — ever since, which is the reason so many have not experienced the kind of victory over sin that the gospel promises.

While there may be some who use "grace" as an excuse to sin, there are also plenty (like those to whom Paul was writing) who genuinely desire to obey God but see no other way of doing so besides the same way as before — *trying*. They have yet to connect the dots between believing in Jesus and obeying him. Therefore, practically speaking, belief and obedience have remained two separate things. While they know they are not *technically* under the law, their obedience continues to depend on a law-abiding, works-based mindset, which keeps them enslaved to sin.

I have no intention to condemn anyone here. This described me for years. My faith was genuine, and I really wanted to be sanctified. But in the moments when I lacked the *desire* to obey, my understanding of God's grace did not equip me with the *power* to obey. Despite my belief in Jesus, my obedience was still almost entirely contingent upon my own willpower (which changed all the time) and not really on my faith in the finished work of Christ. Though *technically* under grace, I was *practically* under the law, and I simply did not know any better. Romans 6-8 is what opened the door for me to see it. Here, Paul's goal is to connect the dots between belief and obedience and to show how grace does exactly what the law was intended to do but never could. In the coming chapters, we will begin to see more clearly how these things are so, but right now, we need to establish a little more context.

A SUBTLER FORM OF WORKS RIGHTEOUSNESS

"But now we are released from the law, having died to that which held us captive…" (Romans 7:6)

It may now be helpful to clarify what is really meant by being "released from the law" and, on the other side of the same coin, what is meant by being "under law" (Romans 6:14). This way, we can determine for ourselves which way we actually tend to operate. Most Christians, I believe, understand these concepts in part, but not entirely. As a result, they live in partial freedom, but not the fullness that God intended for them.

Perhaps the most basic understanding of being *under* the law is that one must obey all or some of the Old Testament Jewish laws — circumcision, Sabbath, festivals, animal sacrifice, ritual washings, diet restrictions, etc. Using this understanding, then, to be *released* from the law is to be free from all those burdensome and no-longer-relevant Jewish commands. (Here is where everyone issues a sigh of relief.) Now, you might reason, we need only to *love* since love is the Great Commandment. But that is just it — love is a *commandment.* Even more, it is the sum, the fulfillment, of God's law, not freedom from it. Anyone who has seriously devoted themselves to perfect love, even for one day, knows that it is an exceptionally difficult standard compared to those old Jewish laws aforementioned. Therefore, let us not fool ourselves into thinking that focusing solely on love inherently frees us from the law. Love *is* the law.

Another way to understand being *under* the law is that one must earn their right standing with God by obeying him. This is the classic understanding of works-righteousness. Logically, then, to be *released* from the law means that we do not have to earn God's favor anymore because we are placed in right standing with him through *Jesus'* perfect obedience and sacrifice. We are, therefore, free from the constant pressure of having to earn God's approval, and we need only to believe in what Christ has done. While this is certainly accurate — and unspeakably wonderful — it is also not the full meaning of being released from the law. Notably, it fails to explain how someone not under the law will actually be *more* obedient than someone under the law.

Or in other words, it fails to make an explicit connection between belief and obedience.

You might argue that God's free gift should simply *motivate* us to respond with loving obedience. The problem is that, though it *should*, it does not always do that (at least not for me)! Even worse, his unearned favor can do the opposite by providing a sense of comfort and safety in the midst of mindful disobedience. In this case, we are back to the problem that many have with Paul's gospel of grace, in that it potentially encourages, or gives a license, to sin. All that to say, this view leaves a very important question unanswered: In those times when we do not feel internally motivated by God's love and acceptance, how does God's grace, or the work of Jesus, still produce obedience in our lives? This question can only be answered when we understand the full meaning of being released from the law.

To be "under law," in the more general way that Paul means in Romans, is for one's obedience to depend on one's own willpower (or you might say *motivation*) to obey. This is righteousness "by works of the law" (Romans 3:20). Under the law, obedience comes about by sheer human effort or works. It is to serve a list of rules and regulations with one's own strength. Or perhaps a little better, it is to love God by *trying* to love him, to receive God by *trying* to receive him, to please God by *trying* to please him, etc. You can call it whatever you like to make it sound better than it is — "surrendering to God," "dying to yourself," "letting the Spirit lead," "resting in his grace," etc. But I think if we are honest, this is often just fancy Christian language for obeying God's commands by doing your best in any given moment. This is, by definition, what it means to live under the law.

Accordingly, to be released from the law means that our obedience no longer depends on our willpower but on our faith in what God has done. It is no longer about having enough motivation. It is about having the right belief. It is not about trying harder but trusting more. As you can probably tell, this will be a common theme for us. Faith *alone* produces obedience, and there is no longer any use talking about willpower.

How exactly this is so will become clearer as we progress through the book, but for now, here is what I hope for you to see. It is quite possible for Christians who believe they have been released from the law to unknowingly continue living under it, desperately trying to obey God out of their sheer willpower, just like any good Jew. According to Paul, this is the exact reason they remain enslaved to sin (and it is the context for the latter half of Romans 7). I deeply believe that this is the way most Christians in this generation have lived, for it is all they have been taught. Do you relate to it at all? Have you ever felt like the Christian life feels like a whole lot of striving and effort — a whole lot of *you?* Have you ever felt like the transformation that it promises is just out of reach? Like no matter how badly you want it, you never seem to want it quite enough? Like no matter how much you love God, you never seem to love him quite enough? If so — and I say this with no condemnation, given that this described me for so long — then you are still operating in a form of works-righteousness (i.e. under the law). I do not mean works-righteousness in the sense that you believe you can *earn your righteous status* by your works. I mean it in the much more subtle sense that you are trying to *grow in righteousness* by your own works, or willpower. But I tell you, there is a better way. The way to righteousness is the way of faith. For "[t]he righteous shall live by faith" (Romans 1:17; see also Habakkuk 2:4; Galatians 3:11; Hebrews 10:38).

LOVE IS THE FRUIT, NOT THE MEANS

By and large, Christians understand very well the idea that they are saved only through faith in Jesus Christ. This is good and true, but it often is missing an important element. When we say that we are saved through faith, most think this to mean that (a) we are reconciled to God through faith, and (b) we will receive eternal life in the future through faith. But what we have often failed to see is that we are *sanctified* through faith, too. Once again, this is Paul's aim — "to bring about the obedience of faith" (Romans 1:5, 16:26). For many Christians, faith is only practical in that it provides the assurance of salvation. It provides the comfort of knowing they are forgiven, in a right relationship with God, and ultimately going to heaven, despite their current state of sinfulness. But do you see how this understanding of faith, for the most part, has to do only with the beginning and the end of the Christian life? What about this whole thing in between called *life?* Through faith, are we only delivered from the *consequences* of our sin, or are we delivered from our *sin*, too?

Is it possible that our daily application of faith looks more Jewish than it does Christian? We believe in God. We pray, worship, and read scripture. We find comfort in being his saved people. We love him, and we want to please him. But when it comes to obedience, the best we can do is try. "Having begun by the Spirit, are [we] now being perfected by the flesh?" (Galatians 3:3)

So how does faith bring about obedience in a way that works cannot? As we discussed in the last section, some may say that since we are not trying to *earn* our salvation, we can freely choose to love God with no strings attached. Or they might say that our relationship with God and his wonderful kindness toward us should stir within us such great love and devotion that we no longer want to sin, and therefore, we choose not to. The problem with each of these is that they leave our daily obedience up to however much love we *feel* in the moment, and we do not always feel it. This is not the "obedience of faith," as Paul describes it, but the obedience of *love*. And love is most definitely a *fruit* of the Spirit, not the *means* to the Spirit.

Think of it this way: You are like a small apple tree, and love is like the apples that you were made to produce. Do you need apples to grow, or do you need to grow to produce apples? Of course, it is the latter. Love is not the *means* to the fruit; love *is* the fruit. Love is not the *way* to righteousness; love *is* righteousness. Love is not the *means* to obedience; it *is* obedience. No wonder obedience has been so hard! No wonder sanctification takes so long and seems so unattainable. We have mistaken the end for the means, and therefore, have had not the means to the end. We have been waiting for more love, but what we really need is more (or more accurate) faith.

To clarify, I am not saying that there is anything wrong with obeying God out of love. This is ideal. When the feeling of love is present and manifesting, it is an awesome grace that makes obedience easy, and we can praise God for that. But we should not solely depend on the *feeling* of love in order to produce obedience to God's commands. That all works wonderfully until you are feeling distant from

God and strongly tempted to sin. If you are going to make use of all the grace you have been given, then you must be grounded in something that is greater than your feelings — the truth. And the truth for every believer is that, despite what we feel at a particular moment, *the love that we need is already and always there* (see Romans 5:5). This is a fundamental truth of the gospel that must be *believed* to be accessed, and we will give much attention to it as we move forward.

While the first half of Romans 7 shows how the law keeps us enslaved to sin, the second half reveals how *even someone who delights in obeying the law* can still be enslaved to sin if they do not understand the grace of Jesus Christ (see Romans 7:18, 22). As we will begin to see in the next chapter, the real problem in the Church is not a lack of love, and the desire for sin lies somewhere other than the believer's heart. Only when we understand this can we begin to see how faith alone delivers us.

Chapter 2

THE SOURCE OF SINFUL DESIRES

We began the last chapter with a very *relatable* passage of scripture — Paul's monologue beginning in Romans 7:14, where he describes his wrestling with and bondage to sin. But then we hinted at the idea that if we truly know and believe the gospel, we should no longer be able to relate to this passage. The gospel has to better than this! To put it bluntly, if Romans 7 is an accurate description of our current spiritual lives, then we are not living the new life of freedom which we have been granted in Christ Jesus. It is proof that we have not learned how to "access by faith… this grace in which we stand" (Romans 5:2). We have been living under law and calling it a state of grace. Despite being free, we have continued living as slaves.

This is always the result of trying to obey God by our own willpower. Only the truth will set us free, and only faith will bring about the obedience and love we so deeply desire. At this point in time, we do not need more love, more discipline, more prayer, or even more grace, for that matter. We need more truth. We need more faith. We need to know how the gospel works.

As we read the rest of Romans 7, I believe these things will become even more evident. And as you will see, this passage lays a great foundation for the gospel. But before we get on to the main takeaway from Romans 7, we must briefly address its most common misinterpretation.

PAUL, THE SLAVE TO SIN?

Starting in verse 14 is where many get lost in Paul's rhetoric: "For we know that the law is spiritual, but I am of the flesh, sold under sin. For I do not understand my own actions. For I do not do what I want, but I do the very thing I hate" (v. 14-15). By changing to the present tense (whereas he had been using the past tense), it appears that Paul has begun to talk about his current spiritual state. But if the reader knows Paul at all, they almost inevitably feel some internal conflict. Could the same apostle who said, "I am not aware of anything against myself" (1 Corinthians 4:4), also have said *years later* that he was still such a struggling wretch? And how could the man who so confidently urged his disciples to "[b]e imitators of me, as I am of Christ" (1 Corinthians 11:1) here be so pitifully defeated in sin? It is, admittedly, a little confusing. But fortunately, we can do far better than merely speculate about Paul's spiritual life. We need only to look at the surrounding passages for our answer.

For example, in verse 14, Paul says, "I am of the flesh, sold under sin." But just earlier in verses 4 and 5, he indicates to his Christian brothers and sisters that they are no longer living in the flesh. Not to mention, he tells them explicitly a couple of paragraphs later that they "are not in the flesh but in the Spirit" (8:9). And what about his being sold under sin? Has he not just spent the entirety of chapter

6 explaining to them that they are dead to sin (6:11), set free from sin (6:7, 18, 22), no longer under the power of sin (6:14)? There is no reason to doubt what he means here. In Christ, they have been set "free… from the law of sin" (8:2) and are no longer debtors to the flesh (8:12). Tell me, were all the Christians in the Spirit, but Paul still in the flesh? Were all the disciples free from sin, but the apostle still enslaved? I can hardly imagine an argument so biblically unsound as this, and we have only touched on the first of twelve verses in this passage. Must we go any further? Is not Paul's rhetoric in this passage completely contradictory to the rhetoric of triumph and victory which he provides to the Church in the rest of chapters 6-8? Unequivocally, it is.

You see, it is quite evident that Paul is not speaking about his current spiritual state. Rather, he is speaking as someone who believes in God, desires to obey him, yet is still living under the law. He is describing the state of slavery that a person who delights in God experiences but does not yet know the grace of Jesus (like, for instance, himself when he was a zealous Pharisee), and therefore remains under the power of sin. He is contrasting this miserable state of slavery with the state of grace and freedom that his believing readers are truly in.

If we miss this point, believing that it describes the state of every believer, the best we will get out of this passage is solace. Indeed, we will read it like one slave saying to another: "I get it, man. Hang in there. It'll all be over soon enough." But the other, more dangerous, possibility is that it will become one of the passages we champion to validate our own pitiful experience. We will go on pridefully about the hard, grueling nature of the Christian life, "humbly" insisting that no one can expect to have any greater freedom than Paul appears to have in this chapter. Anyone who suggests otherwise, we will say, is either prideful or naive. And subtly but surely, having given greater power to sin than to the Spirit of God within us, our gospel will become practically impotent.

However, the moment we recognize that this is not meant to be a depiction of the Christian life, but of the state of someone under the law and not grace, it becomes an amazingly practical passage that will help us to see the gospel in all its beauty.

FLESH AND SPIRIT

We have already learned some very important concepts, but there is one more crucial piece of the puzzle, without which we cannot understand the full extent of our problem, and more importantly, the gospel solution. We have learned that "the power of sin is the law" (1 Corinthians 15:56), but now we must discuss what is the weakness of the law — the *flesh* (see Romans 7:5-6, 8:3). As we are about to see plainly, this is not to be mistaken with our *spirit*. In fact, the weakness within us that sin takes advantage of may not be *in us* nearly as much as we thought. Here lies the final piece that will lead us to the glorious victory of the gospel. "The spirit indeed is willing, but the flesh is weak" (Matthew 26:41; Mark 14:38).

Let us take some necessary time to make an important distinction between our spirit and our flesh. Biblically speaking, these refer to the immaterial and material self, respectively. This is not necessarily to say that the two are separable but distinguishable.[4]

The spirit is commonly described in the Bible as the mind, the inner being, the heart, the soul, etc. You can use whichever term you like; I will continue to use "spirit" and "self" most frequently in this chapter, and in the following chapters, I will use "heart" quite often, as well. This is the *ego*, or the person, which contains my personality and my will. Most importantly for our discussion, this is the "I" that loves God, that repents and believes, or otherwise, the "I" that rejects God and willingly goes after the passions of the flesh. In the Church today, this is what gets most of the negative attention. In other words, if I *feel* empty and depressed, then I determine that *I* am empty and depressed. If I *feel* angry or hurt, then *I* must be angry or hurt. If I *feel* anxious and worried, then *I* need a cocktail. If I have certain

---

[4] I recognize that many Christians have strong and differing beliefs on the nature of "being," and I do not desire here to make a case for my own as I believe it is beyond the scope of this book. The conversation becomes complex and confusing very quickly, particularly because there is such a wide range of words used in the Bible to describe the parts of a person, as well as a variety of meanings for the same words. That being said, one of the best ways to determine whether your paradigm is true is to (1) hold it up to scripture and (2) pray for revelation — not only in that order, but back and forth, back and forth. It is helpful to use the most literal translations of scripture for this process, so that you know which words were actually being used. Consultation of good scholarly resources is always encouraged, if not necessary, since dealing with other languages. Don't dismiss things too quickly, and don't accept them too quickly, either. Humbly seek God for wisdom, and expect him to give it to you. If it makes sense of things that were once confusing, and if it appears to maintain its integrity throughout the whole of the Bible, then you may be on to something. This is the process by which I, personally, settled at the understanding of a material and immaterial self. Fortunately for us, it also happens to be the most simple and intuitive explanation of them all. Isn't it possible — or even, isn't it quite likely — that humans are exactly as we most intuitively perceive ourselves to be: body and spirit?

sexual preferences, they are what *I* prefer. If I continue to struggle with an addiction, then *I* am an addict. If I feel a compulsion toward something, then *I* must want it. If I said something that I should not have said, or did something that I should not have done, then *I* am at fault. If I lack the discipline to pray, then *I* do not love God enough. Etc.

The general assumption is that the corruption, the fallen nature, exists in my *spirit* and is a product of my own will. Thus, it is a reflection of *me*. But as we will come to see, *I* may not always be the problem. Again, as the wise Master said to his disciple, "The *spirit* indeed is willing, but the *flesh* is weak" (Matthew 26:41; Mark 14:38, my italics).

Now, the concept of "flesh" deserves greater attention here as it is a more nuanced word and more widely misunderstood.

First — and this is *not* the most rudimentary meaning of it, but it is prevalent in the New Testament and will be helpful to us later — the flesh sometimes carries the connotation of "human doing," and thus, works of the law. Paul tells the Philippians to "put no confidence in the flesh" (Philippians 3:3), equating it to "a righteousness of [one's] own that comes from the law" (3:9), and contrasting it with "the righteousness from God that depends on faith" (3:9). To the Galatians, he says, "Having begun by the Spirit, are you now being perfected by the flesh [i.e. works of the law]?" (Galatians 3:3). To be born of the flesh (or born *in Adam*) is necessarily to be under the law, having to obey God with one's own strength.

Another helpful example is in Galatians 4 when Paul uses the story of Abraham's two sons — Ishmael and Isaac — to allegorically make this point. Ishmael, he says, was born "according to the flesh," and Isaac was born "according to the Spirit" (4:29). Obviously, Isaac was born *in* the flesh just like Ishmael, but Ishmael was born *according to* the flesh, which means that his birth was accomplished by *human will and effort to bring about God's promise.* Contrarily, that Isaac was born *according to the Spirit* means he was born *by God's doing through faith.* In Romans 8, when Paul speaks about those who "live according to the flesh" (8:5), this is part of the inherent meaning. In other words, living according to the flesh does not necessarily mean that we are *trying* to disobey, as many of us have been taught. In all truth, one can earnestly be striving to obey God while still living according to the flesh. But in the flesh, we are under the law. And despite even our best intentions, we remain enslaved to sin, unable to please God.[5] Why? Because of the "law of sin that dwells in my members [i.e. my flesh]" (Romans 7:23). This leads us to the other, more fundamental, meaning of "flesh."

The flesh is closely related to the body, and I will use the terms "body" and "flesh" interchangeably throughout the book, as does the Bible. It is the nature we were born into, and it is the temple in which our spirits reside. We must not confuse the flesh and the spirit with one another. My spirit describes *me.* My flesh describes the body that I am in.

"Flesh" is the term used for all living creatures on earth, and therefore, it carries with it the connotation of that which is "earthly," "carnal," and "animal" in nature, as opposed to that which is spiritual or heavenly in nature. Given how all earthly creatures are described as "flesh," it is no surprise that obedience to the *passions* of the flesh is what the Bible calls *sin.* It is not okay for us to be "like irrational

---

[5] Paul's short discourse in Romans 8:5-8 is, in fact, the *summary* of his argument in Romans 7, which we will soon read.

animals, creatures of instinct…" (2 Peter 2:12; cf. Jude 10), obeying every impulse as animals do. Perhaps one of the clearest definitions of sin can be found in Romans 6:12:

> Let not sin therefore reign in your mortal body, to make you obey its passions. (Romans 6:12)

It is worth clarifying that, according to Greek grammar, the "its" in the latter phrase can only refer to the "body," not to "sin." Therefore, it should be interpreted like this: "Let not sin therefore reign in your mortal body [or flesh], to make you obey [your body's] passions." We sin when we obey the desires of the flesh.

In the same way that animals have drives and desires which are not the product of a conscious will but the product of their flesh nature, we too have bodily passions which come from our flesh nature and not necessarily our conscious will. The difference between animals and us is that we are to be image-bearers of God, obeying *his* will, exercising *his* dominion, and showing *his* character, regardless of what our flesh would have us do. We are not to be subservient to the body, letting it control us, but servants of God, offering our bodies to him. (see Romans 12:1)

This ought to lead us far away from the heretical conclusion that the body is evil. Some may be quick to label me as this kind of heretic, although I am not. Our bodies are not at all like prisons that we need to escape. Rather, they are like temples that need to be cleansed and re-appropriated to their original purpose. They were created good, manipulated by evil, corrupted by sin, and redeemed in Christ. Just because the second and third of those statements are true does not mean that the first and fourth are untrue. Our flesh is not evil; rather, its *desires* are manipulated by evil to deceive our spirits into sin. We will talk more extensively about how this occurs throughout the book.

Next — and this is very important — the flesh and its passions are not all merely physiological in nature, but psychological, too. This makes sense if you consider the fact that chief among our organs is the brain, in which occurs a wide spectrum of thoughts and feelings, both positive and negative. In a way, the flesh has a "mind" of its own.[6] Along with things like lust, hunger, anxiety, depression, and addiction, it also produces such things (or is vulnerable to such things) as pride, fear, greed, jealousy, and resentment. Again, we know that animals can feel all of these things. This being the case, it is quite easy to mistake this "mind" of the flesh with one's true thoughts and feelings — believing that because one feels it, it is how one truly feels, or because one desires it, it is what one desires, etc. This *can* be true but is not necessarily true. In actuality, there are all sorts of things that occur in our minds, which make us think all sorts of thoughts and feel all sorts of feelings, but that have nothing to do with who we really are, what we actually believe, or what we truly want.

---

[6] Worth noting is that this aspect of the flesh is, on a select few occasions, referred to in the Bible as the "soul" (Greek: *psyche*; see 1 Thessalonians 5:23 and Hebrews 4:12). These passages can be quite confusing, since *soul* is most commonly used interchangeably with *spirit*. By misunderstanding the use of the original language, these passages have led many to believe that the soul and the spirit are two distinct aspects of a person *in addition* to the body. Yet, this conclusion is inconsistent with the rest of Scripture, and I believe it adds much confusion to otherwise simple spiritual truths. In the select cases in the New Testament when *soul* and *spirit* are juxtaposed, the soul is referring to the flesh (or the mind of the flesh) as opposed to the actual person (spirit) inside the body.

I would assume that we all have experienced this many times, whether we have recognized it or not. Think of an occasion when you were genuinely convicted of sin; you repented and determined to do right; you had every intent and desire to move forward in righteousness; and then in no time at all, you were tempted to do the very thing which you had just turned away from. And then, after giving in to the temptation, you felt the exact same grief and conviction as you did you before. So what is going on here? Do you hate the sin or love the sin? Which is proof of what your spirit truly desires — the *sin*, or the *conviction* that follows it? According to Scripture, it is the latter. Assuming a sincerely repentant heart, it was not *you* that desired to sin, but your *flesh*.

> "For I do not do what I want, but I do the very thing I hate... So now it is no longer *I* who do it, but sin that dwells within me" (Romans 7:17, my italics).

The desires of the flesh may appear to be a part of you, but if you confess Jesus Christ as your Lord and Savior, then you must not confuse them with *you*. As I noted above, this is what Christians have done all their lives, but please hear me now. It must stop. It is, quite literally, spiritual suicide. *You* are not your flesh, and your flesh is not always an expression of your spirit or will. If you are going to walk fully in the victory that Jesus has won for you, you must be able to distinguish between your *spirit* and your *flesh*, between *you* and your *body*. It will be a central theme moving forward.

FLESH, OR FALSE SELF?

At this point, we must address what is sure to be a sticking point among some believers regarding the concept of "flesh." There are many Christians who interpret "flesh" (Greek: *sarx*) to mean the old or false *self* which desires to sin, whereas your new and true self does not.[7] In this understanding, the flesh is not material, but immaterial, not physical but spiritual. It is a person and a will, rather than the body in which the person resides. And therefore, every believer has two *selves* dueling inside of them. I would like here to give this viewpoint due attention since I believe it can seriously hinder one's freedom.

The most basic problem we should recognize in this view is that it completely contradicts the inherent meaning of *flesh*, which literally describes the soft tissue of the body.

Second, and perhaps most importantly, Jesus came in the "likeness of sinful flesh" (Romans 8:3). In fact, "he had to be made like [us] in every respect" (Hebrews 2:17) to be able to help us when we are tempted since he also has been tempted. But here is the problem. If we understand the desires of the flesh to be the desires of a sinful self, then either (a) Jesus was a sinner with his own evil desires (see Matthew 15:18-20) or (b) he did not actually come in the flesh, nor was he tempted as we are. Of course, we know that neither of those is true, for he "in every respect has been tempted as we are, yet without sin" (Hebrews 4:15). That being the case, this spiritualized understanding of the flesh

---

[7] This may be partly due to the fact that many modern Bible translations render Paul's words for the "old *man*" as "old *self*" (see Romans 6:6; Ephesians 4:22; and Colossians 3:9), which is somewhat misleading. When he says "man" (Greek: *anthropos*), he is referring to the flesh, but not to a version of yourself, as in, your spirit.

actually threatens the integrity of the incarnation on multiple levels. Not to mention, if we want to learn from Jesus how to overcome the passions of the flesh, it helps to understand what exactly it is that he overcame — not his own desires, but the desires of his flesh.

Next, a very practical problem is that if the flesh and the spirit are two "selves" — one good, one bad — that you must choose between in any given moment, then there must be a *third* self to make the choice, which is intuitively ridiculous. Otherwise, which self do you hold responsible for your actions? Say, for example, you do something that you are not proud of. You later are convicted and desire to repent. In an effort to grow, you think back to the occasion and investigate how you allowed the sin to occur. According to this belief, the old self is responsible for all sin, and the new self is responsible for all righteousness. So first, you think to blame the old self. But if you have any integrity whatsoever, you cannot *really* blame him; he is a sinner just doing his job. And he is not really *you*, anyway. He is the old, false you. So you have no choice but to blame your new and true self since he is the one who is always supposed to do right. It is *his* job to kill off the old self, and he failed. But wait, I thought that all sin came from the old self and all righteousness from the new self? Then how did the new self allow the sin in the first place? By definition, he could not have (or else he does not appear to be very new). You are now back to blaming the old self, and it starts all over.

It is quite a maddening process! And once you finally realize through logic that there must be a third self who truly makes the choices, you see that these other two selves are really just different expressions of *you*. There is not actually a *true* you and a *false* you; there is only one *real* you.

There is not actually an *old* you and a *new* you; there is only one *current* you. Thus, *you* are an ever-changing mixture of old and new, good and evil, righteous and sinful, free and captive, dead and resurrected — however impossible and paradoxical that may seem. This is the only logical conclusion of the dueling-selves theology. It is altogether contradictory to the amazing gospel of Jesus Christ, which says that the *one* you has been made completely new.

I imagine getting to speak to the Apostles in heaven and saying something like, "Hey, when you wrote 'flesh,' did you *actually* mean *flesh*?" Or "When you said 'body,' did you *really* mean *body*?" Stifled by such an obvious question, they would simply say, "Yeah, that is what I meant. How else could I have said it?" Oh, how the devil has twisted the simple meaning of the biblical text! Read it like a child, and you will see that it means exactly what it says. As you are beginning to see now, this is not a matter of mere semantics or personal opinion. In the New Testament epistles, sin is consistently portrayed as obedience to the passions/desires of the *flesh*, the *members*, and the *body*; not the soul, the self, the heart, or the spirit. All that to say, this slight distortion of the term "flesh" has made the original apostolic message nearly incomprehensible.[8]

---

[8] You may wonder how this happened, the spiritualization of "flesh." I do not know for sure, but I believe it is the result of an overreaction to the early heresy of Gnosticism, in which material existence was believed to be evil and inferior to spiritual existence.

Gnosticism's contempt for the flesh led naturally to the conclusion that God did not become flesh, or if he did, that the resurrection of Jesus Christ was not a bodily one. The incarnation and the bodily resurrection are, of course, central doctrines of the Christian confession which needed to be defended, and they were. But as is often the case, the devil uses heresy not only to make people believe one lie — in this case, that material existence is evil — but then to distort the truth that is being defended, creating another

This will become much clearer, I hope, in the following chapters. But for right now, we should recognize the real trouble it causes. If we go on thinking that the flesh is actually part of the self, it renders us incapable of identifying the source of our sinful desires. And knowing not what it is that enslaves us, we cannot understand how Christ frees us. Knowing not what it is that wars against us, we will never know how to fight back. Knowing not what it is that depraves us, we are unable to see how Christ sanctifies us. The Father of Lies would have it no other way.

WILLFUL DISOBEDIENCE, OR SLAVERY?

Now that we see the distinction between the spirit and the flesh, we can easily grasp what is occurring in the latter half of Romans 7. Before reading it again, let us first remember the context. Paul is making a case to the Roman Christians that the law is no match for grace in its ability to bring about obedience. His point is this. As long as we continue living "in the flesh" and "under law," striving to obey with our

---

lie entirely — *that there is nothing corrupt in our material existence, and evil is only in the spirit.* We have tried so hard to preserve the *goodness* in our earthly nature that we have blinded ourselves to the *corruption* within it. What better way for Satan to distort the gospel than to make believers think that sinful desire is still a product of our heart, despite God's work of giving us a new one.

Fear of falling into the Gnostic heresy is the reason that Christians read passages like Romans 7:5, Romans 8:9 or 2 Corinthians 5:16 (which indicate that we are not in the flesh) and determine that the "flesh" about which Paul is speaking must be something other than our material nature, or else Paul appears to be a heretic pushing for disembodied existence. But this conclusion is completely unnecessary to avoid the Gnostic error, and more importantly, it distorts and convolutes the gospel. These passages, which indicate that we are not in the flesh, point to another reality entirely — the *hidden* life in Christ in heaven. We will speak to this more beginning in Chapter 4.

willpower, we will continue under the power of sin *despite our desire to obey*.

As you read the scripture again, notice that Paul describes himself in two distinct parts. There is an "I" who delights in the will of God, and there is another — called the "flesh" (7:14, 18, 25), "members" (7:23), and "body" (7:24) — in which sin dwells and reigns and contradicts what he truly wants. Using the understanding of flesh and spirit from the last section, I will highlight some of these verses, including the appropriate label in brackets.

> "I do what I [spirit] do not want, but I do the very thing I [spirit] hate" (Romans 7:15).

> "For I know that nothing good dwells in me, that is, *in my flesh*. For I have the desire [in my spirit] to do what is right, but not the ability to carry it out" (Romans 7:18, my italics).

> "I delight in the law of God, in my inner being [spirit], but I see in my members [flesh] another law waging war against the law of my mind [spirit] and making me captive to the law of sin that dwells in my members [flesh]… Who will deliver me [spirit] from this body [flesh] of death?" (Romans 7:22-24).

Do you see the conflict? This is not the battle between two selves, but between a corrupted body of flesh and a willing spirit. *Paul is not describing a state of willful disobedience and a need for repentance, but a state of slavery and a need for deliverance.* In fact, he feels this so strongly that twice in the same stream of thought, he says that when he does what he does not want to do, "it is no longer I [spirit] who do it, but sin that dwells within me [flesh]" (7:17,20). Doesn't this sound a lot like the verse I have already quoted twice? "The spirit indeed is willing, but the flesh is weak" (Mark 14:38). A point worth clarifying is that Paul is not overlooking or diminishing the importance of repentance or a change of heart. Rather, he is assuming that it has already happened since he is writing to believers.

> "But thanks be to God, that you who were once slaves of sin *have become obedient from the heart* to the standard of teaching to which you were committed" (Romans 6:17, my italics)

This is my assumption, as well, for those who are reading this book.

The truth is that we have misdiagnosed the problem. When it comes to sin, we too often have wrongly assumed that the culprit is our heart, our will, our spirit, our self. No matter how much we truly hate the sin, we would not dare have the audacity to say, "It is no longer I who do it," despite that these are the very words used by the Apostle Paul! Instead, we say self-deprecating things like, "If only I wanted God more…", "If only I loved him like I should…", "If only I wasn't so [insert insult]…" etc., "*then* I would obey." *What a lie! It is not true! You are murdering the image of God in you!* You *do* want God! You *do* delight in his will! His "love *has been* poured into our hearts"! (Romans 5:5, my italics).

Our failure to see this has led to generations of Christians living in unnecessary condemnation and slavery, waiting and praying for the day that they finally have enough love or willpower in their hearts to overcome sin. Yet this day never seems to come. Faith alone will do the job, in Christ and his finished work, and we will soon begin to see how this is so.

But perhaps the first step to freedom is to recognize that if we have already repented and given our lives to Jesus; if we already delight in God in our inner being; then the desire for sin is not in our *spirits* anymore but in our *flesh* (that is, our bodies)[9]. For repentant believers, sin is not a reflection of our genuine will. Be patient, continue reading, and I think this will become more clear to you. Like Paul, we need to distinguish between the self and the sin and to discern that "it is *no longer I* who do it, but sin that dwells within me." Again, to be clear, this is only true for born-again believers whose spirits are new. An unbeliever's heart/spirit is still contaminated with evil desires. And the point here is not to say that we are not culpable for our sin, but rather to recognize where the source of our sinful passions lie — in our flesh, not our spirits. For the believer, this does not negate the need for repentance; it just changes the way we repent. It does not mean we are unable to sin; rather, it ably equips us to fight against sin. And while this does not yet get us all the way to victory, it is a solid foundation for comprehension and application of the gospel.

---

[9] Once again, I must insist that this is nothing close to Gnosticism. I am not saying that the body is inherently evil, but that it is weak and corruptible. In this case, the solution is not disembodied existence, but redeemed *bodily* existence, restoring its inherent goodness.

Chapter 3

THE FULL RENEWAL
OF THE HEART

The first many years of my Christian life, I thought of myself as pretty much my same old self with a little extra help from God. I would have told you that I believed I had been made new and set free from sin — since this is biblically undebatable — but my understanding of these truths was flawed. I did not *really* believe that I was an entirely new creation. Instead, I believed that I was essentially the same person as before, just with a new "life," or a new direction in life, in the basic sense that I was now following Jesus and destined to be with him forever. Like Jesus' own disciples in their first years with him (prior to his death and resurrection), I had simply chosen to leave my old life behind to go with him. Now with the Holy Spirit, I had him around to teach me, lead me, encourage me, and love me. Nevertheless, I still felt like *me*, the same sinner I had always been, just not wanting to sin anymore. I felt that I was still in the same sinful flesh, only now desiring to overcome it, hoping one day, I might be able to with Jesus' help. But is this all that is meant by "newness of life?"

And regarding my "freedom," I was not entirely sure what it meant, either. It was a lot more like free will than it was like victory. At best, I figured it to mean that my sin no longer had *as much* control over me as it did before. But despite my desire to obey God, I found that I was constantly under the influence of the same sinful passions, too often giving in to the flesh. And I was unable to reconcile the truth in Scripture — that I was free from sin — with the truth about my life. If I was truly free, then why did I still feel enslaved to sin? I could not blame God (although sometimes I did); the problem had to be me. The only conclusion I could come up with was that apparently, I did not want God enough. So once again, I was left waiting for the day that God would finally change me.

I spent years waiting for that breakthrough, praying for that "second" conversion when I would fall madly in love with God and conquer my flesh once and for all. Through these years, I would swing from zeal to disappointment to apathy to conviction, then start the process all over again. I confessed my sins often; I sought help from the body of believers; I prayed for deliverance with fervor; I sought God the best I knew how. And I waited expectantly for a change, until I inevitably grew tired and disappointed in myself, forced to accept once again that this was just the Christian life. This was what God had done for me — he had placed me in a battle that I must fight but could not win, not even with his help. Sure, there was "no condemnation," but there was no genuine sense of victory, either. Not in this life, anyway.

How pitiful! How wretched! How dare we call this a state of grace?! Sin without knowing God, and it hurts but a little. But spit in your Lover's face — day after day — then thank him for forgiving you and tell him you love him, knowing full well that you will do it again. One cannot continue in this state for long, without either beginning to hate themselves or grow numb to their sin. Not surprisingly, most choose the latter. It is simply too painful otherwise. And I tell you, if it were not for the actual grace of God, I would have been left in that hell for the remainder of this life. How many well-intentioned, misinformed Christians are stuck in that same awful state?

I had been reconciled to God through the forgiveness of sins — that much I understood. But now forgiven, what advantage did I have in this new life over my previous state? What exactly is this "grace in which we stand" (Romans 5:2)? I know I had the Holy Spirit, full access to God, and any amount of help I could need from him. But *I* was still *me*. I was still a sinner who, despite my ultimate desire to do God's will, could not seem to do it in the given moment. And in the midst of my temptations, whatever extra help God was ready to provide, I was surprisingly unwilling to reach out and receive. What help is it to be in a relationship with God, or even love him deeply, if whenever temptation arises, I cannot muster up the desire to call on him for help? What good does it do to have the Holy Spirit if I willfully shut him out every time my flesh is aroused? What good is it if my heart delights in God, but my flesh delights in sin, and I am still a man of the flesh? I will tell you, bluntly. It is good for nothing. It is no help at all. As wonderful as it is to be in a relationship with God, this relationship never changed me the way I had been taught that it should.

Then in one short season, everything changed when I learned that the grace I had been looking for had already been given, and more, how to walk in it through faith each day of my life. For years, I had been seeking a renewal of my heart, but as it turns out, I would be "transformed by the renewal of [my] mind..." (Romans 12:2). I did not need to learn how to *do* better; I needed to learn how to *believe* better.

These days, when people ask me how to break free from sin, I will ask them, "What do you think it would take for you to be free?" Almost without fail, they say something like: they need to be more disciplined; they need to pray more; they need an accountability partner; they need God to change their heart; they need to better understand why they act the way they do; etc. Notice what all these have in common. Each is a work *that has yet to be done.* It is unfinished business. And whether they imagine this work to be done is on God's end or their end, the point is that they are left in wait, simply wondering when the gospel will deliver on its promises. I can relate to this. But what we are about to learn is that, by and large, Christians have been waiting for something that has already been done and can only be received by believing that it is true. I assured you of a gospel that sets you free, and it begins by understanding how it already has.

THE WORK OF JESUS

Let's start where we left off in the last chapter. Remember when we made a distinction between the flesh and spirit? That will be very helpful now in understanding what God has done through Jesus for all who believe.

When a person is set on pursuing the desires of the flesh, there obviously must be a change of heart and a turning toward God to live according to his commands. For "[i]f anyone loves the world, the love of the Father is not in him" (1 John 2:15). One must choose to "flee youthful passions and pursue righteousness, faith, love, and peace, along with those who call on the Lord from a pure heart" (2 Timothy 2:22). Otherwise, they have no salvation. I am not, in any way, trying to diminish the importance of this step, which we might simply call *repentance*. In fact, we will give it greater attention in the final chapter. But here, we must come to terms with the fact, once again, that this step *alone* does not equal freedom and victory over sin but leaves us under the power and control of our flesh, despite all our efforts to be good. Even when we desire to do what is right, if we are still in the flesh trying to obey God by our own willpower, then we are not walking in grace and freedom. Romans 7 is the clearest place in scripture that attests to this truth — that to simply want to obey God is not the proper solution for the problem at hand (see Romans 7:22-24). We must *believe* in what God has done through Jesus Christ, our Lord.

In Jesus, God (the Word) was born into the flesh and under the law. He was made fully human — although still God, of course — and therefore required to obey the law by his own strength, resisting and overcoming all the passions of the flesh which were contrary to this. "For all that is in the world—the desires of the flesh and the desires of the eyes and pride of life—is not from the Father but is from the world" (1 John 5:16). The law promised life to all who obeyed (see Romans 7:10) and death to those who did not (see Genesis 2:17). Jesus is the *one* who, by the strength of his own will, fulfilled all the commands of God, successfully conquering the temptations of his flesh, becoming obedient to the point of death, and keeping his whole self (including the flesh) pure and holy. He, therefore, was able to present himself to the Father "without blemish or spot" (1 Peter 1:19). This is what Jesus means when he says, "Do not think that I have come to abolish the Law or the Prophets; I have not come to abolish them but to *fulfill* them" (Matthew 5:17, my italics). He came to live the perfect and sinless life — by works of law — that was required of every human. He came to merit eternal life (in human form/nature) through righteousness. This was not merely a fulfillment of the Jewish law as the scribes and Pharisees understood it, but a fulfillment of true righteousness, which is perfect love, wherein nothing within a person defiles him (see Mark 7:14-23; Matthew 5:20,48).

Now consider the phrase: "the wages of sin is death" (Romans 6:23). When one sins, one owes. But since Jesus did not sin, he did not owe anything. Therefore, death had no power over him. This is why, just before breathing his last, it says that he: "yielded up his spirit" (Matthew 27:50); "gave up his spirit" (John 19:30); and said, "'Father, into your hands I commit my spirit!'" (Luke 23:46). This is also why he said, "No one takes [my life] from me, but I lay it down of my own accord. I have authority to lay it down, and I have authority to take it up again..." (John 10:18) The long short of it is that, although his death appeared (temporarily) to be a win for the powers of evil and darkness, it was the exact opposite. This final act of obedience *completed* Christ's perfection and thus, sealed his victory over sin and death forever. Hence the resurrection. Death could neither take his life nor keep him dead. "God raised him up, loosing the pangs of death, because it was not possible for him to be held by it" (Acts 2:24). Because of his righteousness, he was raised again to life, in a new and glorified human body, in which he is now seated at the right hand of the Father.

Now (and this is where I beg your attention), if we were to stop there — at Jesus' incarnation, death, resurrection, and ascension — then the gospel would be a solo victory for God with no benefit to his people. Jesus would be the only human in heaven forever. None of these things that he so wonderfully accomplished would have any meaning or practical value in the life of his followers. Make no mistake about it, the linchpin of this whole operation is that those who believe "receive the gift of the Holy Spirit" (Acts 2:38). This is more than a friendly relationship with the Spirit; it is *oneness* with the Spirit. For "he who is joined to the Lord becomes one spirit with him" (1 Corinthians 6:17). And from this reality flows nearly every grace in the Christian life.

I say this to make an important point. The work of Jesus is not simply something for us to admire from afar, to stir up the kinds of emotions in our hearts that might then motivate us to repent and obey. If we understand and preach the gospel this way — as merely a motivational tool — we continue under the law that requires us to obey with our own willpower (which we often lack). I am not sure it matters that some preach "grace and forgiveness" over "hell, fire, and damnation." One motivates with love and the other with fear, but both do nothing more than try to motivate hearts of stone. And if we are honest, it does not take long for the masses to grow dull of hearing these motivational speeches. We all know we *ought* to be more affected by

Jesus' work, but the fact is, usually, we are not. Thank God we do not need to rely on motivation any longer. There is more to the gospel; there is more to grace; and we must only believe.

We will eventually get very practical, but we must first devote ourselves to fully understanding what Christ has done for all who believe. The union of God and man is our focus moving forward, and it is multi-faceted. For the rest of this chapter, we will discuss what it means that Christ is *in us*, and then in the next chapter, what it means that we are *in Christ*.

Before we do, I encourage you to read and contemplate Jesus' prayer:

> "I ask… for those who will believe in me through [the] word, that they may all be one, just as you, Father, are in me, and I in you, that they also may be in us, so that the world may believe that you have sent me. The glory that you have given me I have given to them, that they may be one even as we are one, I in them and you in me, that they may become perfectly one… Father, I desire that they also… may be with me where I am, to see my glory that you have given me because you loved me before the foundation of the world" (John 17:20-24).

NO LONGER I WHO LIVE, BUT CHRIST WHO LIVES IN ME

Up to this point, I have not addressed what I imagine to be a major concern regarding what I wrote in the last chapter — that we need to distinguish between the self and the sin.

Or to put it a little differently, we need to recognize that the desires of our flesh — *even those which we act out* — are not a true reflection of our will. I have been saving that conversation for this moment. Here are some of the questions you may have: How do I know if my spirit is truly willing? Can I say, without deceiving myself, that I actually *want* to be free and obey God? Can I say *with integrity*, "It is no longer I who sin, but sin that dwells within me?" How do I discern what is of my flesh, and what is of my spirit?

These questions, admittedly, are quite difficult to answer when one must discern the thoughts and intentions of *their own* heart. But fortunately, this is no longer an issue for the believer since the heart has been "circumcised" by the Spirit of God, himself! (see Romans 2:29; cf. 2 Corinthians 3:3; Acts 7:51; Deuteronomy 10:16, 30:6). To be sure, this was God's promise from long ago that he has fulfilled in all who believe in Jesus.

> "And I will give you a new heart, and a new spirit I will put within you. And I will remove the heart of stone from your flesh and give you a heart of flesh. And I will put my Spirit within you, and cause you to walk in my statutes and be careful to obey my rules" (Ezekiel 36:26-27).

Pay close attention to those words, and you will see that he promised to *remove* the bad heart/spirit and replace it with his own.

This "renewal of the Holy Spirit" (Titus 3:5) does not simply mean that Jesus is *with* us now as if we are basically the same persons as before with just a little extra help from God. No, it means that we have become *one* with God. Our spirits have been joined! His desires are our desires. His will is our will. His character is our character. His righteousness is our righteousness. *Our identity, through and through, is Jesus.* "Or do you not know that the unrighteous will not inherit the kingdom of God?... And such *were* some of you. But you *were washed*, you *were sanctified*, you *were justified...* by the Spirit of our God" (1 Corinthians 6:9-11, my italics).

One of my favorite verses that describes this total transformation is Galatians 2:20:

> "It is no longer I who live, but Christ who lives in me" (Galatians 2:20).

To be honest, I used to think that Paul was speaking here of some heightened spiritual state that he had achieved through many years of hard work and devotion to the Lord so that after dying to himself over and over again to a greater degree each day, he could finally claim that he had completely died and embodied Christ. For me, this meant that I had much more "dying" to do before I could make the same claim. But this is not what Paul is saying. In the context of this passage, Paul was writing about *justification*, which occurs the moment a person believes. He is not describing his state of *maturity*, but his state *since believing in Christ*. He is not boasting of his progress in the faith but teaching the whole Church what they, too, are to believe about themselves. This is not a matter of opinion, nor is it up for debate. Read it for yourself. It is a plain matter of fact. There is one prerequisite for the renewal of your spirit — faith. If you confess Jesus Christ as your Lord and Savior, say it now with confidence: "It is no longer I who live, but Christ who lives in me!" It is not the same old you *plus*

Christ. It is *Christ*. It is not Christ *and* you. It is Christ *in* you. It is not your sin *plus* his righteousness. It is *his righteousness*. Let nothing else but this define your life on earth.

You say, "This is hard to believe! Can it really be true? It does not *appear* to be so." Let me introduce you, believer, to the real thing called *faith*. There is nothing more for you to do but to believe in what he has done. They asked, "'What must we do, to be doing the works of God?' Jesus answered them, 'This is the work of God, that you believe in him whom he has sent.'" (John 6:28-29) Try for even half a day to believe such a magnificent thing, and you will see how "faith in Jesus" means a lot more than you may have been taught.

For practical purposes, this means that there is no longer any reason to wonder who we really are or what we truly desire. It matters not one bit what we *see* or *feel* in a given moment. Sight and feelings are things of the flesh. We are not saved by seeing, nor are we sanctified by feelings. If something is sinful or contrary to the character of God, then it *must* be of the flesh and not from your spirit. No matter how strongly you feel the desire, it is not actually *you* desiring it, but your flesh desiring it, which the Enemy wants you to confuse with your spirit.

> "For the desires of the flesh are against the Spirit… to keep you from doing the things *you want to do*" (Galatians 5:17, my italics).

This verse makes it easy to understand. Whenever we disobey, it is not because we wanted to, rather, it is because the flesh kept us from doing the thing that we actually wanted to do. Our true desires are in alignment with the Spirit who is in us.

Satan wants you to believe that your anger and pride, your lust and your apathy, your greed and your cowardice, your fear and resentment — and all the fruits of such things as these — were birthed from your dirty, rotten, good-for-nothing soul. This is how he keeps you tied to them — by making you believe that you are still this way. But by definition of who you are, sin *cannot* be a reflection of your soul/spirit, for you have become one with the Spirit of Christ in you. If you want to know yourself, the question is always, *Who is Christ? And what does he desire?* If you fall into sin, it is because you are *deceived* into sin, forgetting who you are (see James 1:22-24), and have not yet been perfected in *faith*.

How many times in the New Testament letters are the people of God referred to as "sinners"? Once (James 4:9). How many times does it refer to them *all* as "saints"? Over sixty. This is not an accident. What a tragedy that in the Church today, we cannot speak to one another this way. We save the label of "saint" for the few who appear to deserve it. And then we ignorantly trumpet, "I'm just a sinner saved by grace," with not the slightest clue of what that grace actually entails. We have an identity crisis, and it is because we do not know the gospel. Sinners, take your false humility and throw it out the window. It should not be allowed in our Church. Believers are saints. That is what the Bible says.

My, oh my, how Satan is shaking in his snakeskin boots! His job has been quite easy up to this point, but it is about to get much harder. Now, we are *literally* the continuance of the incarnation. "Or do you not know that your body is a temple of the Holy Spirit within you, whom you have from God? You are not your own..." (1 Corinthians 6:19). And here is why it matters. What Christ successfully accomplished in his own flesh, he will do again in yours, as you learn to walk by faith and identify with him alone. "[W]alk by the Spirit, and you will not gratify the desires of the flesh" (Galatians 5:16).

What was it, I ask you, that made Christ so unshakable in the midst of suffering and temptation? Perhaps it was that *he knew who he was*. With razor-sharp clarity of his identity in God, the flesh could make him suffer, but it could not *deceive* him into sin. Every manifestation of its corruption was only a reminder of who he was *not*, and therefore, what he came to do. Truth was his anchor, and now it is ours, too.

If you confess Jesus Christ as your Lord and Savior, then you no longer want to sin. You no longer desire the things of this world. Your spirit is clean by the Word you have received. It is no longer you who live, but Christ who lives in you.

"How offensive! How ludicrous! You must *work* to get there!" they will tell you. But no, you must work to *believe* that he has brought you there, and the fruit you desire will emerge. It really is *all* by grace through faith. Is this too much to bear? Does it not wreak of the gospel aroma? Oh, but wait, there is more.

Chapter 4

IN THE LITERAL BODY OF CHRIST

If all you understood was Christ in you — and what it *really* means, as we discussed in the last chapter — you would do very well in the life of faith. In my opinion, this is the easiest concept to grasp and the most immediately practical in the life of any believer. Start relentlessly identifying with Christ alone, believing that he has made you righteous, and you will increasingly bear the fruit of righteousness, putting "to death the deeds of the body" (Romans 8:13). The flesh does not define you, and it is not a reliable representation of what is true about your spirit. We do not need to love God more to obey him more. This mindset just leaves us under the law. Instead, we need to start believing that "God's love *has been* poured into our hearts through the Holy Spirit who has been given to us" (Romans 5:5, my italics). We love him all the time, whether or not we feel it in the moment.

In the coming chapters, we will talk more extensively about how to put this into practice. But here, we must look to another important and powerful piece of the gospel — you in Christ. Without this understanding, I believe it is more challenging to see how the finished work of Christ effectively translates into the life of the believer. But with it, we can see quite clearly how Jesus' death, resurrection, and ascension into glory become more than a metaphor, a motivator, or a symbol of hope for our future. His work is not something we simply admire from a distance, but something that has happened to us, too, which has real-time benefits in our everyday life, all of which are accessed by faith in him.

What you are about to read may be a new concept to you, and if so, is liable to some scrutiny and judgment. Anything labeled as "new" usually deserves this kind of reaction, and it at least ought to raise our suspicion. So just to be clear, I do not believe there is anything new about this, but rather, that it is the clear and consistent biblical witness of our salvation. It is, in my own best discernment, an important piece of the *original* apostolic message, which for some reason that I do not know, seems to have been hidden for a long time, though in plain sight in our Bibles. Each reader will have to discern for themselves what is true, but I believe that if one does so humbly and prayerfully, Scripture will speak for itself. This is not some wacky tangent or intellectual trip. It is a foundational aspect of the *kerygma*, the proclamation, the power of the gospel.

IN CHRIST

Let us begin where we left off — that the Spirit of Christ dwells in every believer. When we say that the Holy Spirit dwells *in you*, this ought to be understood as literally *in your body*. It is as true as the fact that *your* spirit dwells in your body. This, then, should lead us to the obvious conclusion that the Spirit of Christ can be in more than one place at a time — not only on earth in every believer, but also in heaven in Jesus' own body. (The Spirit certainly has not left Jesus in order to fill us!) So the Spirit of God is both in heaven and on earth, in Jesus and in us.

Now, remember what we discussed — that "he who is joined to the Lord becomes one spirit with him" (1 Corinthians 6:17). Well, if we are truly one with the Spirit who dwells in Jesus' own body as well as ours, then doesn't it make sense that we, too, dwell in our own bodies as well as his, on earth as well as in heaven?[10] If "Christ in you" means him in your body via the Holy Spirit, then it only makes logical sense that "you in Christ" means you in his body via the Holy Spirit.

You may wonder how exactly this is so, technically speaking. Although I have my own belief, I cannot teach it with confidence. I am perfectly comfortable leaving room for a little mystery here. Perhaps your spirit *itself* is there, in the most literal way possible. Perhaps it is not. Perhaps you are there *via Holy Spirit* with whom you, the Father, and Son are all one. Or maybe you are in him like a branch connected to a vine, and it is impossible to determine where one ends, and the other begins. "I am the vine; you are the branches. Whoever abides in me and I in him, he it is that bears much fruit..." (John 15:5). Whatever is the case, here is what really matters at the moment. It would be a mistake to say that we are not *really* there, for in this truth, and from this perspective, the gospel comes to life, and the Scriptures begin to make sense.

---

[10] I might also suggest there is something to explore here about the nature of unity and oneness within the Church, which is the Body of Christ. Perhaps, in fellowship, believers share more of their lives together than what meets the eye.

The Bible has plenty to say about this. It is no problem at all if you are not fully on board yet, but at this moment, I would ask you to partake in a simple thought experiment. As you read the following examples, read them from the perspective of being currently in Jesus' body in heaven. Take time to sit with it and pray for understanding, believing that he will give it to you in time.

God "has blessed us *in Christ* with every spiritual blessing in the heavenly places" (Ephesians 1:3, my italics).

God has "raised us up with him and seated us with him in the heavenly places *in Christ Jesus*" (Ephesians 2:6, my italics).

"For *in him* the whole fullness of deity dwells *bodily*, and you have been filled *in him*" (Colossians 2:9-10, my italics).

"[Y]ou were also raised with him through faith in the powerful working of God, who raised him from the dead" (Colossians 2:12).

"[Since] then you have been raised with Christ, seek the things that are above, where Christ is, seated at the right hand of God. Set your minds on things that are above, not on things that are on earth. For you have died, and your life is hidden with Christ in God. When Christ who is your life appears, then you also will appear with him in glory" (Colossians 3:1-4).

Can one, in any real sense, be raised with Christ into heaven, currently seated with him at the right hand of God, and not be in Christ's risen body? How else could this be so? Where else would we be? How else should we explain being *in him* at this very moment? The way that I see it, given what the Bible has to say about this, either we are literally in him (just as he is in us), or else we have not, in reality, been raised with him.

The central theme in the book of Hebrews is, in fact, this very thing. Jesus, the great High Priest, has gone into the real Holy Place, into the presence of the Father in heaven, and his *bodily* presence there now is our means of access to the Father — of course, by the Spirit whom we share (see Hebrews 4:14-16; 6:19-20; 7:25; 8:1-2; 9:11-12, 24; 10:19-22; 12:2, 22-24). "For *through him* we... have access in one Spirit to the Father" (Ephesians 2:18, my italics). In other words, only because *he* is there are *we* there, too. And there, since we are literally clothed in him, we are clothed in glory and perfection (see Hebrews 10:14) and can approach the throne with great confidence. This is "the grace in which we stand" and which we "access by faith" (Romans 5:2).

This is also why Jesus says to his disciples before his departure, "In my Father's house are many rooms... And if I go and prepare a place for you, I will come again [via Holy Spirit?] and will take you to myself, that where I am you may be also" (John 14:2-3).[11] And, "No one comes to the Father except *through* me" (John 14:6, my italics). These

---

[11] It is worth noting that the only other time in the Gospel of John when he uses the term "my Father's house" is John 2:16, when speaking of the temple that he had just cleansed. Just a few verses later, he says "Destroy this temple, and in three days I will raise it up" (John 2:19). Then the writer comments that "he was speaking about the temple of his body" (John 2:21).

verses have often been interpreted to be speaking only about the afterlife. But the rest of chapter 14 makes a good case for the fact that Jesus is speaking of the time after he ascends into heaven and sends them the Holy Spirit.

> "I will not leave you as orphans; I will come to you. Yet a little while and the world will see me no more, but you will see me. Because I live, you also will live. In that day you will know that I am in my Father, and you in me, and I in you" (John 14:18–20).

This is not only a future reality for believers but a current reality, which comes with many benefits. It means more than just a new home or location, and even more than access to God. It means a new life and new nature *in God*, and therefore freedom from the law and the flesh which once held us captive to sin.

JESUS WAS BORN AGAIN

To understand more fully the significance of being in Christ's body, we must better understand what actually happened to Christ regarding his incarnation, death, resurrection, and ascension.

To start, let us reflect upon the Cross and the Resurrection. Concerning these events, it is important to recognize that they were bodily in nature. In other words, Christ's spirit — the *person* of Christ, the Word himself — did not change at all when he died and was raised. He remained God; he kept his spirit; he remained perfect and pure; etc. It was not his heart, or spirit, that changed, but his *body of flesh* that was put off in death and put back on — in glorified fashion — in the resurrection. Following the pattern of Paul's discourse in 1 Corinthians 15:35-57 (which I encourage you to read now), Jesus died in weakness but was raised in power (see also 2 Corinthians 13:4); died in a natural body, but was raised in a spiritual body (see also 1 Peter 3:18); died in Adam, a man of dust, but was raised in God, a man of heaven.[12]

Of course, Paul is describing specifically the bodily resurrection that *we* will experience. But it is inferred within the context of the chapter — and it is a basic premise of the gospel — that this is the same sort of change that Christ underwent, from being in the flesh just as we are, to being resurrected in glory. In fact, that is the whole point. What happened to Christ will happen to us. He is the forerunner, the first of his kind, a new race, a new type of human. He is the "second Adam," and we believers shall follow (see 1 Corinthians 15:20-23; Acts 26:23, Romans 8:29).

Next, you might wonder, wasn't Jesus already from heaven? Yes, and he was God, and *in* God, the whole time that he was on the earth. But his *body* was of the earth — a body of flesh, just like ours (see John 1:14; Colossians 1:22; Hebrews 2:17; 2 John 7). While the fullness of God dwelt in that body (see Colossians 1:19 and 2:9), his body was not of God but of man. Although he was from heaven, his *bodily* nature was not heavenly but earthly like ours. This is the meaning of the incarnation. In taking on our human nature, God became *just like us*. Then, in his resurrection, he obtained a new bodily nature that was not earthly but heavenly; not perishable, but imperishable; and he returned

---

[12] Please recognize, again, that none of this describes a change that occurred within the Spirit of Christ, but the change that occurred to *body* of Christ. It speaks of bodily nature, not identity or personhood.

to where he came from. In just a moment, we will see why this matters, but let us briefly consider another important scripture:

> "That which is born of the flesh *is flesh*, and that which is born of the Spirit *is spirit*" (John 3:6, my italics).

Here, Jesus is not contrasting the two parts of a person — flesh and spirit — which we discussed in the second chapter. Rather, he is contrasting two kinds of nature, both of which are physical and bodily, but of different realms. In other words, someone who "is flesh" is of the substance of the earth, and someone who "is spirit" is of the substance of heaven. Someone who "is flesh" has the nature of man, and someone who "is spirit" has the nature of God. It makes sense, then, why "flesh and blood cannot inherit the kingdom of God" (1 Corinthians 15:50), but only those who are born of the Spirit (see John 3:3, 5). Our earthly bodies were made for the earthly realm. They cannot access the spiritual realm. Therefore, a change of bodily nature, from flesh to spirit, must occur in order to be with God *bodily* in his kingdom.

From the beginning, humanity was *destined* for this, but it had to be merited, or earned, through perfect obedience. By law, anyone who failed to obey God would die in the flesh and never obtain the new nature, thereby failing to enter the kingdom of God and have eternal life (see Genesis 2:17). Even before Adam and Eve ever sinned (despite having the breath of God in them), they were still from the dust of the earth, not from heaven; still with a natural body, not a spiritual one (see 1 Corinthians 15:44-49; Genesis 2:7). God could dwell in their realm, but they could not dwell in his. Therefore, contrary to some popular belief, humanity did not start with its perfect and final nature, then lose it. Rather, we started with a *destiny* and then failed to obtain it.

And here is where Christ comes in.

"For Christ also suffered once for sins, the righteous for the unrighteous, that he might bring us to God, *being put to death in the flesh but made alive in the spirit*" (1 Peter 3:18, my italics).

Notice in the verse above how it states that Jesus, in his death and resurrection, made a transition from flesh to spirit, just like he said was necessary to see the kingdom of God. The phrase "made alive in the spirit" is very interesting and deserves our attention. First, you might wonder if "spirit" refers to Holy Spirit[13]. We know that Jesus was made alive *by* the Holy Spirit (see Romans 8:11), but it does not make a whole lot of sense to say he was made alive *in* the Holy Spirit. So that appears to be a non-option. Next, we might consider it to mean that after "being put to death in the flesh" — that is, after putting off his body — Jesus' own spirit/self was simply raised apart from his body. But we know better than this, for he was raised bodily (e.g. Luke 24:39). In terms of how he was "made alive," it would make no sense at all to speak of his spirit apart from his body. Therefore, this explanation also seems inadequate.

In the third possibility (which is the one that I endorse), "in the spirit" does not refer to the person of the

---

[13] This is often a possibility, and vice versa, since the original Greek was written in all capital letters, leaving it up to the reader to discern its intended use.

Holy Spirit, nor the spirit/self of Jesus. Rather, it refers to the *realm*, and therefore the *nature*, in which Jesus was raised. Just as "flesh" refers to the body in this passage, so does "spirit." He was put to death in one bodily nature but made alive in another. In this new and glorified body, he could eat and drink with his disciples on earth (e.g. Luke 24:41-43; John 21:12-13), appear out of nowhere in the midst of locked rooms (see John 20:19), as well as ascend into heaven (the spirit realm) and dwell at the right hand of the Father.

This is the kind of "spiritual body," which Paul juxtaposes with our "natural body" in 1 Corinthians 15:44. It refers to the spiritual/heavenly nature of God, which those who are saved receive from him. It is in contrast to our earthly nature. It is divine in origin — incorruptible, eternal, immortal, and without the passions of the flesh. Only in this nature can one enter the kingdom of God. "[T]his is why the gospel was preached even to those who are dead, that though judged in the flesh the way people are, they might live *in the spirit* the way God does" (1 Peter 4:6, my italics).

According to this interpretation of 1 Peter 3:18, in the resurrection, Christ himself was born of spirit, or *born again* (see John 3:6). That statement should only offend us if we misunderstand what "born again" means, thinking of it as an inward renewal of the heart/spirit. Thankfully, we have already determined that Christ did not experience this kind of renewal, but a bodily renewal. In its most basic essence, to be "born again" is not to receive a new heart (though that is certainly a part of it for us), but to receive a new nature. Therefore, when Christ was born again (i.e. resurrected), he did not receive a new heart, but a new human body — not of flesh, but of spirit; not of man, but of God.

The fact that Jesus was born again is why he is referred to as "the *firstborn* among many brothers" (Romans 8:29, my italics) and more pointedly, "the firstborn *from the dead*" (Colossians 1:18, my italics) and "the firstborn *of the dead*" (Revelation 1:5, my italics). Here, it is quite plain that Jesus' resurrection is described as a *birth*. It was a birth into the spiritual realm from which he came, except this time not only as God but as man. He did this not for his own sake — for he was already divine — but for the sake of humanity who failed to obtain it for themselves. Now *in him*, we benefit from the work he has done.

IS THIS ALL JUST A METAPHOR?

At this point, you might be wondering what this means for us *now*. It is true that we must wait for *our* resurrection bodies, which we will not receive until Christ returns. But in the meantime, we are not without the power of his resurrection. For remember, we are *in him*, in a very real sense.

This is, in fact, what baptism represents. Just as we receive Christ by receiving the Holy Spirit into ourselves, Christ receives us into himself through the Holy Spirit with whom he also is one. We are literally baptized *into* Jesus, and therefore, into his death and resurrection. Here are some verses that make the point.

> "Do you not know that all of us who have been baptized *into* Christ Jesus were baptized into his death?" (Romans 6:3, my italics).

"We were buried therefore with him by baptism into death, in order that, just as Christ was raised from the dead... we too might walk in newness of life" (Romans 6:4; cf. Colossians 2:12).

"For in one Spirit we were all baptized into one body" (1 Corinthians 12:13).

"For as many of you as were baptized *into* Christ have put on Christ" (Galatians 3:27, my italics).

The predominant understanding of what actually occurs in a believer's conversion and/or baptism usually includes the receiving of the Holy Spirit and some sort of change within the person. It is widely accepted that there is an old life that is left behind and a new life that is begun and that these are somehow connected to the death and resurrection of Jesus. But the clarity usually ends there, leaving one to inevitably wonder, *Have I actually died? If so, then how, and how did Jesus' death cause me to die, too? Is this all just one big metaphor?*

We cannot really blame anyone for asking the question. After all, as we have already discussed, Jesus did not die a *spiritual* death, but a *bodily* death. And his resurrection was a bodily one, too. This should cause us to speculate how it is that we have *actually* been crucified with Christ (see Romans 6:6 and Galatians 2:20). Is not death, by definition, the putting off of the *body*? (see 2 Peter 1:14). Yet even after baptism, we remain in our bodies. The cognitive dissonance is inescapable. Ask almost any Christian today to explain how it is that Jesus' death and resurrection effectually killed them and made them new, and you will see what I mean. It is likely that any explanation of their own "death" and "new life" they can offer does not in any way capture the essence of Christ's death and resurrection, which were bodily events.

But if we take into consideration the idea of being *literally* in Christ — like in his body — it starts to become easier to see. From this perspective, we are not in the flesh at all. Perhaps you are thinking to yourself, "Yes, I am," as you look down at your two fleshy hands. But then you are not thinking from the heavenly perspective of being in Christ, with whom your true life is now *hidden* (see Colossians 3:1-4). You are walking by sight, not by faith. In *his* body (not our own), we have died to the flesh and been raised in the spirit. We have received our just punishment for sin — death by crucifixion. We have also received his just reward for righteousness — the divine nature. We did not *spiritually* "die" like him; we died his very own *bodily* death (see Romans 6:3). That is to say, we "died... through the body of Christ" (Romans 7:4). We were not metaphorically crucified *like* him; we were crucified *with* him (see Galatians 2:20) as he hung on the Cross. Only because we are in his body was he able to "[bear] our sins in his body on the tree, that we might die to sin and live to righteousness" (1 Peter 2:24). Only because we were "baptized into Christ" (again, think literally) as Paul says we were in Romans 6:3, could we be "crucified with him in order that the body of sin might be brought to nothing, so that we would no longer be enslaved to sin" (Romans 6:6). His body is now ours, just as our bodies are now his. And in his body, we have been "*born again* to a living hope *through the resurrection of Jesus Christ* from the dead*" (1 Peter 1:3, my italics). In other words, we have been born again through *Jesus* being born again — not yet in our bodies, but his. Hence why it is a "living hope."

We discussed in the last chapter the circumcision of the heart by the Holy Spirit, but this circumcision is also described in another way.

> "*In him* also you were circumcised… by *putting off the body of the flesh*… having been buried with him in baptism, in which you were also raised with him through faith in the powerful working of God, who raised him from the dead" (Colossians 2:11-12, my italics).

Do you see how a believer's death and new life are real bodily events? In Christ, we are quite literally a new kind of creature, no longer of the flesh, because he is no longer of the flesh.

> "From now on, therefore, we regard no one according to the flesh. Even though we once regarded Christ according to the flesh, we regard him thus no longer. Therefore, if anyone is *in Christ*, he is a new creation. The old has passed away; behold, the new has come" (2 Corinthians 5:16-17, my italics).

So consider all the following terms: "born again" (1 Peter 1:3, 23), "born of God" (1 John 3:9, 5:1), "born of the Spirit" (John 3:3, 6), "regeneration" (Titus 3:5), "newness of life" (Romans 6:4), "new creation" (2 Corinthians 5:17, Galatians 6:15), and "firstfruits of his creatures" (James 1:18). These are all a description of the new nature we have *in Christ*, which is conveyed to us now through his Holy

Spirit, who is within us. They correspond to us becoming "partakers of the *divine* nature, having escaped from the corruption that is in the world because of sinful desire" (2 Peter 1:4, my italics).

For the believer, these have *already* occurred in Jesus' body but have *not yet* occurred in our own, since we obviously have not yet died and been raised in our own bodies. The fact that scripture says over and over again that we have died and been raised through *his* death and resurrection makes no sense whatsoever from the perspective of our own flesh. But it makes perfect sense from the perspective of our being in him. "As he is so also are we in this world" (1 John 4:17).

All this to say, if we have imagined our life "in Christ" to be some sort of metaphor, let us do so no longer. This is no mere symbolism as I once supposed it was. When Christ says, "This is my body, which is given for you" (Luke 22:19, c.f. Matthew 26:26; Mark 14:12; 1 Corinthians 11:24), he means that it is the very vessel through which we have died and been raised to new life, transferred from the darkness to the light. If the story of Noah's ark corresponds to our baptism (see 1 Peter 3:21), then Noah represents the only righteous man, Christ, and the ark represents his body, which carries us safely through the waters of judgment and into the new creation.

All this to say, the "born again" experience, which has been so inaccurately propagated as a one-time decision and a ticket to heaven, is vastly more profound and amazing than it has often been described. It seems the furthest some have gotten is to call it a relationship with God, which is wonderful and true, but still lacking. It is more than a relationship; it is a new life defined by *oneness* with God. It is not an addition to the old self, but a new creation entirely. It is not an ever-changing mix of old and new, of true and false, of sin and righteousness. It is death and resurrection in a single moment — putting off the old nature (flesh) and putting on the new (spirit). It is liberty and victory, now, not later. It is an immediate change in the unseen realm, where at one moment, we are in sin, and the next, we are in Christ. At one moment, we are unholy, and the next, we are a holy dwelling place for God.

"[T]he mystery hidden for ages and generations [has now been] revealed to his saints" (Colossians 1:26). It is "to unite all things *in him*..." (Ephesians 1:10, my italics). It is "Christ in you, the hope of glory" (Colossians 1:27). It is that the two have become one — Christ and his church (see Ephesians 5:31-32). Now, in Christ, God has given us a new and *unseen* reality in which to live, and therefore, a new perspective from which to operate.

NOT IN THE FLESH

Remember, in the second chapter, we discussed the problem with our flesh. Remember also, Paul crying out, "Who will deliver me from this body of death?" (Romans 7:24). Well, now we know the answer. Our spirits were enslaved to sin through our bodily passions. What was God to do? Give us the body of Jesus as a vessel for death, resurrection, and newness of life. This "newness" is not only a renewal of our spirit but a new *nature* in Christ — God's very own nature — which is free from the corruption that we were originally born into.

"For the law of the Spirit of life has set you free *in Christ Jesus* from the law of sin and death" (Romans 8:2, my italics).

The "law of sin and death" to which Paul refers here is a *law of nature* within the body of flesh (see Romans 7:18, 23). This natural law of sin is why "[t]hose who are in the flesh cannot please God" (Romans 8:8) *even if they desire to please him.* But now *in Christ*, we are "partakers of the divine nature" (2 Peter 1:4), and this new nature has a new law — not sin and death, but righteousness and life. Once, we were dead branches, cut off, with no source of life. Today, we are connected to the Vine, and his new life gives us new life, defining who and what we are.

Believers are now to walk by faith according to this new life of freedom and victory that is found in Christ. In doing so, the power of his resurrection is conveyed through the Spirit to our mortal bodies now (see Romans 8:11, 13). We are to "walk not according to the flesh but according to the Spirit" (Romans 8:4). We have spoken of this concept some already — that we are not to identify with the thoughts and feelings of the flesh. But this becomes even easier when we realize that, in Christ, we are no longer even in/of the flesh.

"You, however, are not in the flesh but in the [s]pirit, if in fact the Spirit of God dwells in you." (Romans 8:9)

Just like 1 Peter 3:18, which we discussed earlier, when Paul says here that we are "in the spirit," he is not referring to the Holy Spirit, but to the *spirit realm* into which we have been raised in Christ. Because Christ is in the spirit, we are in the spirit, since we are in him. And the Holy Spirit within us is the guarantee that this is so.

Moreover, Paul's point is not to say that we are no longer technically in our earthly body, nor that we have already experienced our own bodily death and resurrection. He is saying that our life in our own flesh is no longer our true life (see Colossians 3:3), and therefore, it is not the *perspective* from which we are to live. Most importantly, it is an identity statement that permits us to believe what we cannot yet see.

> I have been crucified with Christ. It is no longer I who live, but Christ who lives in me. And the life I now live in the flesh I live by faith in the Son of God, who loved me and gave himself for me (Galatians 2:20).

Notice in this verse that Paul does not deny the fact that he still lives in the flesh, despite that he claims to have died to it (cf. Galatians 5:24). But he says, "the life I now live in the flesh I live *by faith in the Son of God...*" My point is this. We do not have to pretend, in the name of "faith," that our own bodies have already died or been resurrected, despite the obvious reality that this has yet to occur. On the other hand, we should not reduce the work of Christ to merely a renewal of heart when it is more. There is only one solution. The life we now live in the flesh, we are to live from a different perspective — that is, *in Christ* by faith. Like Paul, we are to live according to the unseen reality, where we are risen with him in the spirit realm and no longer in the body of flesh.

It goes without saying that our new life in Christ, to quite a great extent, remains unseen. There is much that is true about us *in him,* which we simply cannot observe through our earthly lens, or perhaps, which may even seem to directly oppose what is easily observable. Therefore, if we are to effectively walk in this new life and capitalize on the power of the gospel, we can only do so by faith, which is "the conviction of things *not seen*" (Hebrews 11:1, my italics). Our faith is what will bear the fruit of the heavenly truth.

This leaves each believer with a choice in every moment. Do we live as if the Holy Spirit is a nice little addition to our otherwise earthly nature and old life? Or do we live as if Christ is, in fact, our new life, nature, and identity? Do we live according to the unseen reality, where in Christ, we have died to sin and been raised to righteousness, with total freedom and victory? Or do we live according to what we see, feel, and experience in the flesh — sins, failures, flaws, brokenness, etc.? Are we defined by Christ's strength and glory, or are we defined by our own weakness and depravity, no better than our most recent sin or deepest wound? Will we walk by faith, or will we walk by sight? Will we set our minds on the Spirit or set our minds on the flesh?

It takes no faith whatsoever to say that we are still in the body of flesh. It is a nearly incontestable truth to anyone with a pair of eyes, common sense, and a trace of humility. We need not deny this reality, but we would do well to ask what kind of fruit comes from focusing on it. Do we not have a higher reality to live by? Do we not have a new and better life to put on? These only describe the life we can see with our natural mind, through our worldly lens, and we "are not of the world" (John 15:19; cf. Colossians 2:20). "[O]ur citizenship is in heaven" (Philippians 3:20). Thus, if we have no other perspective through which to view ourselves, except that which is based on what we can see and feel, we will undoubtedly miss out on our wonderful new life in him.

It takes faith to say, "I have died to sin." Initially, it may even feel like a lie. But it is as true as the fact that Christ was crucified because your new life is *in him*. And when we live according to, or believing in, this new life and nature which we cannot immediately see or feel, we will find ourselves inevitably dying to sin, for it is simply no longer who we are. "So you also must consider yourselves dead to sin and alive to God in Christ Jesus" (Romans 6:11). It takes faith to say, "I am no longer in the flesh, but in the Spirit," when a look in the mirror tells you otherwise. But once you begin believing it is true, then the flesh will miraculously lose its power over you. "From now on, therefore, we regard no one according to the flesh… if anyone is in Christ, he is a new creation. The old has passed away; behold, the new has come" (2 Corinthians 5:16-17).

By faith, heaven is manifest on earth, and Christ is manifest in you. As you live by faith through Christ in heaven, Christ will increasingly live through you on earth. "In this the love of God was made manifest among us, that God sent his only Son into the world, so that we might live through him" (1 John 4:9).

Before we move on, I feel the need to stress that the truths we have discussed in this chapter (and the others, for that matter) will do you little to no good if you do nothing more than think about them intellectually. I urge you — meditate on them, pray for wisdom, and allow them to penetrate your heart. There is certainly far more to explore here than the little we have covered in this chapter (see

Ephesians 1:3). Boldly approach the throne through Jesus, and give thanks to God for what he has done. Marvel at him in the Holy Place, rejoicing that he is in you and you are in him.

Chapter 5

THE TRUE MEANING OF ATONEMENT

In our quest to understand the gospel and grow in faith, there is perhaps nothing with greater potential to hinder us than guilt, shame, and condemnation. We are going to deal with that in this chapter. Satan wants nothing more than to keep you feeling dirty and unworthy, despite the fact that you are forgiven. In fact, he will gladly allow you to have the forgiveness of sins, for there are plenty of ways that he can use this knowledge against you. But there is one thing that he knows will forever give you the upper hand — the knowledge of what God has done with these sins which he has forgiven.

Satan is content for you to believe that God *calls* you beautiful, as long as you do not actually believe that you *are* beautiful. He is content for you to believe that God *declares* you righteous, as long as you do not actually believe that he *has made* you righteous. He is content for you to believe that God willingly *overlooks* your sin, as long as you continue believing that it is still there. He will stop at nothing to distort your image of yourself, to make you believe that the way God sees you is not actually the way you are.

Satan wants you to feel like a wife whose husband tells her she is beautiful, but it does not really matter because she does not see herself the same way. For he knows that if you cannot see what God sees, then you will never be able to give yourself to him fully. You will "protect" God from yourself, choosing *for* him not to be loved. You will project your insecurities onto God, presuming his love and his compliments to be little more than kind lies. And even if you know — as an intellectual fact or a doctrinal position — that he loves you, you will never truly understand why or how or to what extent.

The bedrock of our faith, as it applies to our daily lives, is the atonement of our sins through Jesus Christ, our Lord. There is nothing — and I mean *nothing* — that is a more necessary foundation for our spiritual growth. The Cornerstone has been set. Now we must begin where Christ finished.

THE ATONEMENT GOATS

In the Old Testament, we learn of something called The Day of Atonement, or Yom Kippur. Once a year, the high priest of Israel would enter the Holy of Holies — the innermost place in the tabernacle/temple — to atone for all the sins of the people. It was here that God's presence would "appear in the cloud over the mercy seat" (Leviticus 16:2) to receive the offerings for their sin, which were administered by the priest on Israel's behalf.

Christians, of course, no longer observe this day, nor do we offer sacrifices for our sins, in general. As was the case with many things under the Jewish Law, the Day of Atonement was just "a shadow of the good things to come instead of the true form of these realities" (Hebrews 10:1). Jesus, himself, is our Great High Priest who "has entered, not into holy places made with hands, which are copies of the true things, but into heaven itself, now to appear in the presence of God on our behalf" (Hebrews 9:24). He is the true and final atonement for our sins, forever making us right with the Father and providing us constant access "behind the veil."

Even so, there is still much to learn from the old Jewish ritual, for it provides some great insight about what *atonement* actually means for us today and how exactly it has been accomplished once and for all through Jesus. It is a very powerful thing. The detailed instructions for this annual tradition are found in Leviticus 16, and then the New Covenant comparison/parallel we will use is found primarily in Hebrews 9-10.

Before we get into it, it will be helpful to define a couple of things.

The Hebrew word for "atone" (*kaphar*) means "to cover, remove, or erase." Atonement is a common biblical theme, especially in the Old Testament. It relates to the idea of cleansing the people from sin to remain in right standing with God. This was, in fact, the very purpose of the Day of Atonement. "For on this day shall atonement be made for you to cleanse you. You shall be clean before the LORD from all your sins" (Leviticus 16:30).

Next, we must understand the importance of blood. (This clue will be very handy when we begin to talk about the blood of Christ). God told Israel that "the life of every creature [literally, *all flesh*] is in its blood" (Leviticus 17:14).

The word translated as "life" here is *nephesh*, which also means "breath" and "soul," and it was understood to be the animating life force within every living creature. In this way, it is closely related to (and often used interchangeably with) the Hebrew word *ruach*, which is translated as "spirit," "breath," and "wind." So, according to Jewish theology, the spirit/soul of humans is found in (or at least represented by) the blood, and it is distinct from the body of flesh. This is why, after Cain killed Abel, God told Cain, "The voice of your brother's blood is crying to me from the ground" (Genesis 4:10). The actual person (spirit) was believed to be in the blood.

Regarding atonement for sins, God said, "I have given [the blood of animals] for you… to make atonement for your [*nephesh*], for it is the blood that makes atonement by the [*nephesh*]" (Leviticus 17:11; cf. 17:14, Genesis 9:4). Since animals were naturally without sin, their blood represented a *purity of life*, which was able to act as a covering (atonement) over Israel's sinfulness, effectively making the people clean.

Now, back to the Day of Atonement. First among the offerings that were required was one bull. The bull was sacrificed, and its blood used to atone for the sins of the high priest so that he would be clean and able to stand before God while performing the rest of his duties. Therefore, in our New Covenant parallel, there is no need for a bull since Jesus was without sin.

Next among the offerings were two male goats, which were reserved for the sins *of the people*, each goat serving a unique purpose. The high priest would "cast lots over the two goats, one lot for the LORD and the other lot for Azazel [meaning unknown]" (Leviticus 16:8). The first would be killed, and then its blood would be sprinkled over various objects and places within the tent of meeting to "cleanse it and consecrate it from the uncleannesses of the people of Israel" (16:19). Notice again the purpose of the blood — *to cleanse.* Or another word with almost an identical meaning is to *purify.* "Indeed, under the law almost everything is purified with blood…" (Hebrews 9:22).

Contrary to common belief, the *punishment* for Israel's sins was not being taken out on this goat by means of its death, but rather the *purity* of this goat's life was being *transferred to Israel* by means of its blood (since the life is in the blood). "[F]or it is the blood that makes atonement *by the life*" (Leviticus 17:11, my italics). This understanding of how the blood was used can also be seen in the fact that it was not the people, themselves, who were sprinkled with blood on the Day of Atonement, but the "the tent and all the vessels used in worship" (Hebrews 9:21). These objects did not need to be punished; that would be silly. They needed to be washed, cleansed, purified.

Also worth noting is the fact that this sacrifice was not really a gift from the people to God to appease him; rather, it was a gift from God to his people to cleanse them. Hence, God said, "*I have given it to you… to make atonement for your souls…*" (Leviticus 17:11, my italics). God has always been very gracious.

Now under the New Covenant, it is not enough to say that Jesus simply died for us to take our punishment. He did that and more. Fulfilling the role of this first goat, his perfect and sinless life is transferred to us by means of his blood, making us *perfectly clean* before God and purifying our conscience (see Hebrews 9:14 and 10:22). As I stated before, in Jewish thought, the blood carries the soul/spirit.

Therefore, what was once somewhat of a symbolic act in ancient Israel became a very real thing in Jesus. To be sprinkled with Jesus' blood is to be made one with his Spirit. Never before had there been such a fitting sacrifice for mankind. Since animals do not possess a human soul/spirit, their blood could not truly purify the spirit of man, only the flesh. "For it is impossible for the blood of bulls and goats to take away sins" (Hebrews 10:4). Jesus, on the other hand, shared in our flesh *and* blood. Therefore, the offering of his Spirit has purified (in spirit) those who have received it (see Hebrews 9:13-14). We will come back to this idea shortly.

The second goat (also known as the "scapegoat") is the one that endured the punishment, and it was actually kept alive. As the high priest stood before God with the live goat, he would lay his hands on the goat's head and confess over it all the sins of the people. This also was referred to as "atonement" (see Leviticus 16:10), for he was *covering* the goat in sins. This goat would then *bear the iniquities* of the people in/on its flesh as it was sent outside the camp, off into the wilderness to Azazel[14]. While the meaning of *Azazel* remains unclear, the obvious effect of sending the goat into the wilderness still remains. It signifies the *complete removal of sin from Israel.*

---

[14] There is some debate about the meaning of "Azazel," given that it is found nowhere else in Scripture besides Leviticus 16. That being said, it is found in another piece of Jewish literature, and the meaning there is quite interesting. In chapter 10 of the Book of Enoch (which is an intertestamental Jewish work), we read of the whole earth being corrupted by the teachings of one fallen angel, named Azazel, to whom God ascribes all sin. This sounds a lot like Satan. If these two instances speak of the same character (which I, personally, believe they do), then the conclusion would be that this goat would carry the sins of Israel into Satan's domain (hell), never to return.

It probably goes without saying that Jesus fulfills the role of this goat, too. For he bore our sins in his body of flesh and took them straight to hell where they belong, away from the presence of the Lord (see Hebrews 9:28; Isaiah 53; 1 Peter 2:24). Every time we confess our sins, this is where they go — onto his flesh, not ours. "By sending his own Son in the likeness of sinful flesh and for sin, he condemned sin in the flesh..." (Romans 8:3). They are dealt with, punished, and forever removed from God's sight. "For I will forgive their iniquity, and I will remember their sin no more" (Jeremiah 31:34). Thus, God has forgiven *and* forgotten, as if we never sinned at all. Again, I must remind you that this is no mere symbolic gesture. Those who are *in him* (think of this in the literal sense) have put off the body of sin, having died through his death (see Romans 6:6 and 7:4). We *have been* condemned in the flesh, just not our own. Jesus is more than a substitute; he is a vessel for vicarious death and new life. Since "one has died for all, therefore, all have died" (2 Corinthians 5:14).

Do you see what is happening here? Where is the sin? What does atonement *really* mean? Does God simply overlook our sin, even though it is still there? Or does he deal with it altogether?

Notice what the old system could *not* do:

"According to this arrangement, gifts and sacrifices are offered that cannot *perfect the conscience of the worshiper*..." (Hebrews 9:9, my italics).

"[I]t can never, by the same sacrifices that are continually offered every year, *make perfect those who draw near*" (Hebrews 10:1, my italics).

"For it is impossible for the blood of bulls and goats *to take away sins*" (Hebrews 10:4, my italics).

"And every priest stands daily at his service, offering repeatedly the same sacrifices, which can never *take away sins*" (Hebrews 10:11, my italics).

Here, we can see quite clearly what is the meaning of atonement. While it certainly includes the *forgiveness* of sins (see Hebrews 9:22, 10:18), the *removal* of sin is the ultimate picture. Atonement is only complete if sin is wholly removed.

Read now how this has been accomplished through Christ for all believers.

"For if the blood of goats and bulls, and the sprinkling of defiled persons with the ashes of a heifer, sanctify for the purification of the flesh, how much more will the blood of Christ, who through the eternal Spirit offered himself without blemish to God, *purify our conscience* from dead works to serve the living God" (Hebrews 9:13–14, my italics).

"But as it is, he has appeared once for all at the end of the ages *to put away sin* by the sacrifice of himself" (Hebrews 9:26, my italics).

"[W]e *have been sanctified* through the offering of the body of Jesus Christ once for all" (Hebrews 10:10, my italics).

"For by a single offering he has *perfected for all time* those who are being sanctified" (Hebrews 10:14).

Do not get too riled up yet. We need not claim to be *perfect* (in the sense that there is no more growth to be had). We must claim to be *pure* — i.e. free from a sinful conscience — given that we are walking in faith and humility. More importantly, the point that I am making is this. The Bible says not only that we are forgiven but also that we are *not guilty*, that we are *clean*.

To be sure, it is quite possible to be forgiven yet still guilty or "dirty." This is the way that I thought of myself for most of my Christian life. My debt was forgiven, but not really paid. Or even if it was paid, I just kept incurring more. God loved me and forgave me, but he did not often delight in me. He gave me his Spirit, but *I* stayed somewhat rotten. He removed sin's punishment but left its stain. I was pulled from the mire but still covered in filth. I was not condemned, *technically*, but I could feel his constant disappointment and anger (*unless*, of course, I had been particularly "good" that week). Can you relate?

It seemed that all anyone could tell me is *Don't be so hard on yourself, God forgives you, nobody is perfect*, etc. Or otherwise, I was just told to pray that God would rid the sin from my heart. But no one ever told me that I was *clean* in the truest sense. If only I had read my Bible for myself, prayed for understanding, and taken its words to mean what they mean, I would have learned these truths a long time ago!

It is one thing to stand before Lord *forgiven*. It is another thing entirely to stand before him *clean*. It is one thing to be allowed permission to approach the King, despite that I am still covered in stench and dung. It is another to approach him boldly and confidently, washed clean and clothed in his royal garments. "I will greatly rejoice in the LORD; my soul shall exult in my God, for he has clothed me with the garments of salvation; he has covered me with the robe of righteousness..." (Isaiah 61:10). "And the angel said to those who were standing before him, 'Remove the filthy garments from him.' And to him he said, 'Behold, I have taken your iniquity away from you, and I will clothe you with pure vestments'" (Zechariah 3:4).

Church, how could you be guilty if the atonement was successful? What more must God do to remove your sin? There is only one way to the Father, and it is *through* the Son *by* the Holy Spirit. You cannot possibly get there without being beautifully washed and clothed along the way. As you stand before the Judge, you owe nothing at all (see Colossians 2:14). You are not simply a debtor who has been let off the hook. Rather, the account has been settled, and there is no debt to be seen. You are innocent as a dove, blameless as a lamb. You are justified in his own righteousness, drenched in his own blood, renewed in his own Spirit, recreated in his own nature. "Who shall bring any charge against God's elect?... Who is to condemn?" (Romans 8:33-34). If anyone is accusing you, it is Satan the Accuser, and he does so with *lies*. If there is one thing that the Serpent does not want you to know, it is that you are clean, clean, clean, pure, pure, pure, new, new, new, by the precious blood of Jesus, which has washed you white as snow.

I think it is safe to say that the majority of the Church currently believes that God graciously chooses not to see our sin, even though it is still there. But let me ask you this, believer. Can Truth personified call me clean when I am not? Can Truth, himself, choose to see something that is not true? Is this not straight blasphemy?! "What God has made clean, do not call common" (Acts 11:9). God is not a liar, nor is he blind. If he does not see sin, it is because it is not there (see Jeremiah 31:34 and Hebrews 10:17). What, then, must he be looking at? He is looking at the heart (see Acts 15:8-9).

Why is it, then, that there is "now no condemnation for those who are in Christ Jesus?" (Romans 8:1). It is not merely that we are forgiven despite our remaining sin. *In Christ*, we are not even in the "body of sin" (see Romans 6:6-7, 8:9). And in the Spirit, "the righteous requirement of the law [is] fulfilled in us" (Romans 8:4). Yes, our sin has been dealt with, all evil removed from our hearts. The passions of the flesh may wage war as they do. But thank God we have been delivered, and that is no longer who we are.

"Therefore, brothers, since we have confidence to enter the holy places by the blood of Jesus... let us draw near with a true heart in full assurance of faith, with our *hearts sprinkled clean from an evil conscience* and our bodies washed with pure water" (Hebrews 10:19-22, my italics).

SINLESS PERFECTION?

There has been a centuries-long debate in the Church about whether or not sinless perfection is attainable in this life. To be honest, I believe that both sides have missed the boat. The argument itself shows that we have not properly understood either (a) the atonement or (b) the way to perfection. Having reduced the atonement to the forgiveness of sins, or at best, a partial removal of sin, our focus has been on ridding the *remaining* sin from the heart. It is quite unbelievable how we have gone back and forth about whether this state of sinlessness can possibly be attained when, according to the gospel, we already have it by faith. We mistook a sinless spirit, a pure heart, to be the *end* of the Christian life, when actually it is the *beginning*, apart from which we cannot bear fruit. It is God's seed, his Holy Spirit, our new identity in Christ, which our faith must entirely cling to in order to bear the fruit of righteousness.

This is not to say at all that God's work in us is finished. Rather, it is to say that his work in us begins when we start believing he has removed sin from our hearts. It is also not to say that we are already perfect and will never sin again. Instead, it is to demarcate the *source* of sin and righteousness.

Thus far, I hope to have made it overwhelmingly clear that the heart, or the spirit, is what God has made new and pure, righteous, and holy. This is the *person* within the body of flesh, and the two must be distinguished. For the flesh, itself, still has sinful "passions... which wage war against your soul" (1 Peter 2:11). Notice, it is not the other way around. "[T]he desires of the flesh are against the Spirit... to keep you from doing the things *you want to do*" (Galatians 5:17, my italics). "[B]ut if by the Spirit you put to death the deeds of the body, you will live" (Romans 8:13).

So you see, to put to death the passions of the flesh and abstain from sin, we must first know the truth that those sinful passions are no longer our own. They are born in our flesh, and the only reason we obey them is that we are deceived into thinking they come from our spirit. Hence the need to renew our *minds* (see Romans 12:2, Colossians 3:10,

Ephesians 4:23). As long as we continue to believe that we still have sin in our spirit, we will be unable to walk according to the sinless Spirit, with whom we have been made one (see 1 Corinthians 6:17). "You know that he appeared in order to take away sins, and in him there is no sin" (1 John 3:5).

WHAT ABOUT 1 JOHN 1?

This sort of conversation almost always leads the Church back to one particular scripture — 1 John 1. There are certainly others that are relevant, but this is one that has been notoriously divisive. It is worth our time to look at it now.

> V. 7 - "But if we walk in the light, as he is in the light, we have fellowship with one another, and the blood of Jesus his Son cleanses us from all sin."

> V. 8 - "If we say we have no sin, we deceive ourselves, and the truth is not in us."

> V. 9 - "If we confess our sins, he is faithful and just to forgive us our sins and to cleanse us from all unrighteousness."

> V. 10 – "If we say we have not sinned, we make him a liar, and his word is not in us" (1 John 1:7–10).

As you might imagine, verses 8 and 10 are most often used as an attempt to destroy any argument that a Christian can be without sin. It is one of those, like Romans 7, that is ignorantly misinterpreted, taken out of context, and then used to defend and glorify the work of the devil — all in the name of Jesus. These dissenters of holiness doctrine are under a satanic delusion that they are somehow "protecting the sanctity of Jesus" by insisting that he cannot sanctify, "preserving the integrity of the gospel" by limiting its power. They are so intent on maintaining their doctrinal position that they have become blind to the truth that is right in front of them. If you are one of these people, I assure you, the Lord will keep you blind in your sin if you do not humble yourself before him and pray that he reveals to you the plain truth within his Holy Scripture.

Look at the context, beginning in verse 7. "[I]f we walk in the light... the blood of Jesus... cleanses us from all sin." Tell me, how can one be cleansed from sin and still have it? He does not say we are cleansed from the *stain* of sin, or the *effect* of sin, or the *consequence* of sin. He says we are cleansed from *sin* itself. And not some of it, but all of it. As we discussed in the last section, this is the essence of atonement. It makes no sense whatsoever to speak of being cleansed from something if it still remains.

So when he says in verse 8, "If we say he have no sin, we deceive ourselves..." he is speaking of acknowledging our depravity *apart from Jesus*. It is true that "all have sinned and fall short of the glory of God" (Romans 3:23). To be sure, no level of spiritual maturity — not even the state of perfection itself — would negate one's basic need for God's saving grace. Everyone has sinned. If we fail to acknowledge this, claiming to have a righteousness of our own, then by definition, we are walking in the darkness, not the light. But as he says in verse 9, when we acknowledge this reality, Jesus forgives us and cleanses us from *all unrighteousness*. How foolish it would be, after having been cleansed, to then go on believing that we are still dirty! It is worth noting, as well, that cleansing is something different than forgiveness. John was not being redundant in saying that God forgives us *and* cleanses us. His point is to express the completion of the atonement, the full removal of sin, for all who have turned from darkness to the Light.

Just as we cannot walk in the darkness and have fellowship with the Light, neither can we walk in the Light and remain in darkness. For "God is light, and in him is no darkness at all" (1 John 1:5). Hence, if we are truly in him, then there is no darkness in us. We can also relate this back to some things we have already discussed. If, for example, "[i]t is no longer I who live, but Christ who lives in me" (Galatians 2:20), then how could I still claim to have sin in me? Would I not have to renounce this glorious thing that God has done? Would I not have to deny his grace and subdue my faith? "So you also must consider yourselves dead to sin and alive to God in Christ Jesus" (Romans 6:11).

In the next verse (1 John 2:1), John writes: "I am writing these things to you so that you may not sin. But if anyone does sin, we have an advocate with the Father, Jesus Christ the righteous." Notice John's explicit intent for what he just wrote — that they *may not sin*. And does he presume that they will, or does he presume that they will not? He says, "*if* anyone does sin," not "*when* everyone sins." Is it not shockingly clear that they had a different perspective than we do today? Should we call John a heretic for suggesting that they could actually go on without sinning? If one of his disciples came to him a month later and said, "John, thanks to your instruction, I have not sinned!" do you think John would balk at this claim? Do you think he would yell, "Liar! Liar! The Truth is not in you!" Or do you think he would celebrate that the man was walking in the light and that the cleansing blood of Jesus was having its intended effect?

Perhaps an analogy is needed to help us understand John a little better. Imagine that the goal was for you to get to my house. In this case, saying that you have no need for my address is like saying that you "have no sin" (1 John 1:8), or no need for cleansing, even though you most clearly do. This would be very prideful and stupid. You would simply be deceiving yourself, and you would never be able to make it here. Nor would I have a reason to give you the address, under the pretense that you do not need it. But if you told me that you did not know the address, then I would give it to you. Problem solved. After having received it, you would forever *rely* on the information that I gave you, but you would not *need* it in the same way as before. It would be untrue for you to tell people that you got here on your own and that you had no need for my help. But it would be just as untrue to say that you were still in need of my address as if I never gave it to you at all.[15] Apply this to 1 John, and you will see what I mean. If you confess your sins to God, acknowledging your need for his grace, he solves the problem by removing all your sin. He makes you clean and pure as he is. And after this occurs, it is just as untrue to say that he did not cleanse you as it is to say that you had no sin from which to be cleansed.

Here is our real problem. We have one sinful thought, and we conclude, "I guess I am still not righteous." The flesh gets the best of us, and we decide that God's word is not true. A brother acts according to the flesh, and we say, "See, you are a still sinner, not yet perfected." But the proper response would be to say, "Don't be deceived. That was not

---

[15] See John 14:4-6 for an interesting parallel.

who you are. Remember and believe that you have been cleansed." We think that if you confess your sins, then you are admitting to still being unclean. But actually, confession is the very confirmation of our newness and our cleanness. It is a reaffirmation of who we truly are in Christ. It is, itself, evidence of our heart's true desires, proof that he has made us righteous and pure. But if you are unsure at all about the state of your own heart, the Bible says confess, and you will be made clean and righteous. After that point, you must start to believe it is so.

I want to be very clear again about something. Our *flesh* is not yet perfected. For that, we await our resurrection body. In the meantime, its passions can still rage on and wage war against us. In this sense, our perfection is an ongoing work, not yet complete. But what does Paul say? "[W]e regard no one according to the flesh" (2 Corinthians 5:16). Therefore, we must categorically reject that the flesh's desires are our own. For to live according to the flesh (or to identify with the flesh) is to inevitably deceive ourselves back into sin, rendering the atonement practically ineffective. "For to set the mind on the flesh is death..." (Romans 8:6).

And there is yet another point on which I must make myself clear. It is not that we should take no responsibility for our sins, nor that we should think it is impossible for us to sin. Rather, we must accurately identify *the source* of our sinful passions and, in the case that we do sin, why it happened. If our spirits have been renewed, then sinful desire comes from the *body of flesh*, and the reason for sinful action is *deception*. If we sin, it is not because we truly wanted to do said thing, but because our spirits were deceived into identifying with the passions of the flesh. And if we have any doubt at all whether our hearts are truly pure, we can always purify them by faith that we are washed in the blood.

There is no need for guilt or condemnation; only a need to think better and grow in faith. We are "transformed by the renewal of [our] mind[s]" (Romans 12:2). In this sense, also, we have not yet been perfected. It is not so much that we have been defiled, but deceived. We have not been in sin but in infancy. We have not been evil but ignorant. We have not been wicked but weak. We have not been complicit but gullible. I am speaking, of course, to those who have already been cleansed by the blood. We do not need more cleansing now; we need more faith. But those who willfully continue in deception prove themselves to be transgressors (see Galatians 2:18).

Whether or not sinless perfection is attainable in this life, at least in the sense that we have meant it for so long, may not be as important as we thought. It is true that sanctification is a process in one sense, for we must mature in our thinking (or grow in faith) to walk by the Spirit and put to death the deeds of the body (see Romans 8:13). But the process will never happen (let alone be completed) if we are not focusing on the *finished* work of Jesus, who has already cleansed us, removing sin from our hearts. This is the reason we have been lacking in the spiritual fruit. We will never bear the fruit of righteousness if we do not believe he has made us righteous. "For whoever lacks these qualities is so nearsighted that he is blind, *having forgotten that he was cleansed from his former sins*" (2 Peter 1:9).

Make no mistake. You cannot walk in the Light if you are walking by sight. Believe that you are clean and righteous by the Spirit of God within you, and this truth will set you free like you never imagined was possible.

Chapter 6

HOW FAITH
BRINGS ABOUT OBEDIENCE

In the first chapter, we asked the question, *How does faith bring about obedience in a way that works cannot?* We now have a great foundation to answer that question. In faith, we live according to a new reality — an entirely new state of being — in which obedience to God's commands is no longer in tension or conflict with our nature but an aspect of it. In faith, we stop allowing the thoughts, feelings, and actions of the flesh to dictate what we think about ourselves, for we are no longer in the flesh but in Christ. Instead, we let the word of God tell us who we are, despite what we may see and feel in a given moment. For "if anyone is in Christ, he is a new creation" (2 Corinthians 5:17). Faith entails much more than believing God loves you, that Christ died for you, and that you are going to heaven. It entails more than just trusting in his good will and the help of the Holy Spirit in you to do better. Faith looks into the unseen realm and takes hold of the new *you,* which has been "created after the likeness of God in true righteousness and holiness"

(Ephesians 4:24). Faith says confidently, "I have died to sin and been raised to righteousness." It does not say, "I need more love," but rather, "The love of God is within me." It is not persuaded and stifled by the opposing evidence of the flesh, but instead, relentlessly identifies with the new life in Christ, where sin and shame have been conquered forever.

ROMANS 6

Let's apply this to some scripture and bring it to life. Romans 6 begins with the question, "Are we to continue in sin that grace may abound?" (v. 1). As we discussed in the first chapter, Paul's readers wanted to know how obedience was relevant in the context of God's grace. It seemed to them like it was just a license to sin without fear of punishment. Like many still today, they understood the initial grace in the life of a believer to be the forgiveness of sins and the free gift of eternal life, but not much more than that. If this were the case, then it truly would not matter whether a person flees from sin and pursues righteousness, for sin would not at all be opposed to God's saving grace. The more we sin, the more God forgives. No wonder they were offended at the gospel of grace! No wonder they insisted on the practicality of the law to bring about obedience. And no wonder so many Christians today go on sinning like it is nothing. It all comes down to what we believe about grace, or, more specifically, the grace which a person receives initially through faith in Jesus Christ. So this is what Paul sets out to do — explain God's grace and how it crucifies sin. Here are some highlighted verses from his response.

"How can we who died to sin still live in it?" (v. 2).

"We know that our old [man] was crucified with [Christ] in order that the body of sin might be brought to nothing, so that we would no longer be enslaved to sin" (v. 6).

"For one who has died has been set free from sin" (v. 7).

"For the death [Christ] died he died to sin, once for all, but the life he lives he lives to God. So you also must consider yourselves dead to sin and alive to God in Christ Jesus" (v. 10-11).

"But thanks be to God, that you who were once slaves of sin have become obedient from the heart to the standard of teaching to which you were committed, and, having been set free from sin, have become slaves of righteousness" (v. 17-18).

"But now that you have been set free from sin and have become slaves of God, the fruit you get leads to sanctification and its end, eternal life" (v. 22).

I cannot tell you how many times I read this chapter before I ever understood what was really going on here. For years, my only takeaway was that it is not okay for a Christian to keep sinning. With a slightly condemning tone (even though I knew I wasn't *technically* condemned) I heard Paul saying: "Sin?! How could you?! After all God has done for you…" At times, this led to subtle doubts regarding my salvation. Of course, I would remind myself that I am saved through faith, not works, but then I could not help but wonder whether my faith was even real, given the sin that still remained in my life. Other times, this was just one more chunk of scripture to put in the "stop sinning" bucket — relevant for those who abuse God's grace, but not relevant for me and others who actually want to obey God. In reality, though, Paul is saying something much different and more helpful.

As you look again at the verses above, pay close attention to the language Paul uses to describe their condition. Notably, he does not view their freedom from sin as something still to be obtained, but rather, something that was accomplished by Christ on the cross and their baptism into his death. It is a finished work. Many Christians have mistaken this freedom from sin, which Paul describes, to mean simply that we now have "free will," or the freedom to choose whether or not to sin. There are a number of problems with this view, but most importantly, it misses the obvious point that Paul makes, which is that in Christ, we have *died* to sin. If this is actually true, then is it even possible to live in it? Further, we have become *slaves* of God and righteousness. Can we be slaves to righteousness, and at the same time, free to sin? The language Paul uses here strongly suggests something more than the freedom of choice. In fact, I would argue that it expresses a state which is directly opposed to our general notion of free will.

Contrary to popular belief, when Paul says in verse 2, "How can we who died to sin still live in it?" he is not appealing to the heart of the believer, suggesting that if you are grateful for God's grace toward you, you will choose to obey him out of love. As we spoke in the first chapter, this actually just leaves us in a form of works-righteousness, continuing to rely on our own willpower to do what is right. Instead, he is appealing to the *unseen reality* of the believer, suggesting that if you understood correctly what God has done for you in Jesus, you would clearly see how you are unable to continue in sin. Why? Because it is no longer who you are. When Paul says, "how," he means *literally* how? He means that if you have truly died to sin (and believe it), it is not possible to continue living it. What is dead is dead. As it says in 1 John 3:9, "No one born of God makes a practice of sinning, for God's seed abides in him; and he *cannot* keep on sinning, *because* he has been born of God" (my italics).[16]

To be sure, then, our death in Christ — which happened when we first believed and is marked by our baptism — does not merely result in a "turning toward Jesus," but a complete change in our state of being. It is death to our flesh and new life in God. It is freedom from sin and slavery to God. The mechanism that propels the believer toward sanctification is not the will within that person to overcome the flesh and do what is right, but the faith within that person to believe that, in Christ, God has crucified the flesh and caused them to be born again as slaves of righteousness, sons of obedience, children of God, etc. From this new identity or state of being — and living by faith that it is true — comes the "fruit [of] sanctification and its end, eternal life" (Romans 6:22).

---

[16] The more natural translation of the Greek in 1 John 3:9 is "...and he cannot sin..." As John's letter is very black and white throughout, this appears to me to be the better translation, more in alignment with his overall message. He is making the connection between the ideas that (a) in God/Jesus there is no sin (see 1 John 3:5) and (b) His seed abides in us (see 1 John 3:9). Therefore, those who are born of him *and walking/abiding in that truth*, cannot sin.

Therefore, regarding the initial grace received by every believer, the forgiveness of sins and "newness of life" (Romans 6:4) go hand in hand. It is not forgiveness now, and then freedom later, or even freedom gradually. It is a package deal when one believes in Jesus Christ and receives his Spirit. By definition of God's grace, one cannot be both forgiven and still enslaved to sin. Therefore to receive this grace (aware of what one has received) and then to mindfully choose a life of sin, believing or hoping that one is still forgiven, is actually to reject this grace entirely. To be born of God and then to willfully choose the old life in the flesh is a complete renunciation of one's status and identity as a child of God. To "go on sinning deliberately after receiving the knowledge of the truth" (Hebrews 10:26) ought to be a terrifying thing for anyone who understands what they have done. So the gist of Paul's argument in Romans 6 is that grace far exceeds the law in its practicality to bring about righteousness (or obedience) in the life of a believer, and when grace is *properly* understood, it gives neither excuse nor power to sin.

Now, it is important that we know how to appropriately process and apply what Paul is saying. We have a horrible tendency to subconsciously repackage the word of God to make sense of what we can see, rather than take it for what it actually means.

Paul says, "How can we who died to sin still live in it?" (Romans 6:2). If you are like me, your natural mind thinks, "How can we have died to sin if we are still living in it?" Or "How can we, who live in sin, have died to it?" Do you see the difference? For Paul, the given is that through Jesus, we have died to sin. Therefore, he determines that we cannot continue living in it (not that we *shall* not, but that we *can* not). But according to our natural minds, the given is that we still find ourselves sinning, so we determine that we must not yet have fully died to sin, despite the gospel telling us otherwise. (If what I just said does not yet make sense to you, I urge you to read it again until it does. It is very important.) Paul's eyes are on Christ, his finished work, and our new life in him. Ours are on ourselves, the unfinished work, and our old life in the flesh. Maybe it is time that we take Paul's lead and learn to "walk by faith, not by sight" (2 Corinthians 5:7).

IDENTITY DRIVES ACTIONS

It is a fact of human life, and well-researched in the field of psychology, that our sense of identity drives our actions. What we believe about ourselves in terms of our inward being is the driving force of our outward doing. Here lies much of the power of the gospel. To be clear, this is far more than the power of positive thinking, and it is much different from the sort of philosophy which says we can forge our own identity or re-create ourselves. The Christian is not a self-made man, nor a product of humanistic optimism. Rather, God has caused us to be reborn, literally, through the death and resurrection of Jesus Christ — no longer in the flesh, but in the Spirit; not of natural descent, "but of God" (John 1:13). It is not simply that he has convinced our old self to follow him and love him, but that "[t]he old has passed away... the new has come" (2 Corinthians 5:17). We have been given a new life, a new identity, and a new nature altogether, and for this to translate to our daily lives, we must first begin to see ourselves in this new Light.

If liquid water thought itself to be ice, it would not freely move about. If steam thought itself to be liquid water, it would never rise from its place. But each knowing the truth about their current state without question, they obey the properties of that state as if there were no choice at all. The same goes for people. We obey the properties of whichever state we believe we are in. If a person grows up thinking they are intellectually impaired, they will exert far less effort into learning than if they believed they were capable of learning anything. If someone is convinced they are unhealthy — not just as a temporary state, but as this *type* of person — it will be nearly impossible for them to establish a routinely healthy lifestyle. They may be able to go against the grain of their identity for a while, but unless they begin to identify as a healthy person, the new lifestyle will not be sustainable. If a child is taught they are rotten, all their desires to be otherwise will be overshadowed and overpowered by the seemingly inescapable identity to which they have been subjected. "Should I be kind and obedient today?" they will think to themselves. "It sounds nice to stay out of trouble and make some friends, but unfortunately, that is too hard for me. That is just not the kind of child I am."

This applies to the Christian life, as well. Using the example from Romans 6, Christians who mistake God's grace for mere forgiveness, and thus, think of themselves still as sinners, are certain to go on sinning. But those who see God's grace for what it is, and thus, "consider [themselves] dead to sin" (Romans 6:11) *as they truly are in Christ*, will naturally stop sinning. This is not to say that a true Christian will never sin again; rather, it is to recognize that when we do, it is not due to a faulty self but to a false understanding of self. If after sinning, we think to ourselves, "I must have wanted to do that; there is still something wrong with me," then we have misidentified ourselves with the flesh, with which we are no longer to identify (see Romans 8:9; 2 Corinthians 5:16; Colossians 2:11). The truth is, we did not sin because we wanted to, but because we *thought* we wanted to, nor because we had to, but because we *thought* we had to. Thus, we were deceived. For Christians, failure to grow and mature in the way of holiness, or to obey in any given moment, is nothing more than a failure to see (or believe) who and what we truly are. Or else it is evidence that they are not born of God.

If you are a Christian and you feel condemned by this, or hear me blame you for not having enough faith to be free from sin, then you are missing the point. I am not saying it is your fault; I am saying it is not *you*. I am not pointing my finger at you; I am pointing you toward Christ. If someone in the flesh and under the law can say, "it is no longer I who do it, but sin that dwells within me" (Romans 7:17, 20), then how much more can the believer, who is no longer in the flesh but one with Christ, rightfully dissociate from the sin with which they once identified? In Christ, you are a child of God, made entirely new in his image — how could you be condemned? Satan wants to shame and discourage you for still struggling with sin and not having enough faith to change. But no amount of faith can add to or take away from who you already are in Christ; it can only help you bear the fruit of, and live in alignment with, the new and true you. Satan's tactic is to get your eyes off of victory and onto your sin because he knows that the only thing standing between you and transformation is the knowledge that you have been transformed. God has done it. You must fight to believe it.

Having been born of God, there is now only one way to know yourself truly — know Jesus truly; one way to see yourself clearly — see Jesus clearly; one way to evaluate your character — evaluate Jesus' character; one way to measure God's love for you — measure his love for the Son. For Christ *is* your new life (see Galatians 2:20; Philippians 1:21; Colossians 3:4; etc.). In this new life, the compulsion to obey and love God arises out of one's sense of being, which has already been won through Christ, and therefore, can only be received by faith. This is the "obedience of faith" (Romans 1:5 and 16:26), which Paul contrasts with the obedience that comes about through one's own striving or willpower. By God's grace, we have been re-created "in true righteousness and holiness" (Ephesians 4:24), and this will become increasingly evident in our lives, the more we believe it is true.

BEING VS. DOING

I have heard many sermons, and even preached some myself, on the topic of "being versus doing." The classic scripture for this subject is the story of Martha and Mary, sisters who had Jesus into their home for dinner (see Luke 10:38-42), although there are plenty more. A common takeaway is the importance of spending time *being* with Jesus — usually pertaining to more contemplative activities like prayer, scripture, worship, or recreation — over and against *doing* things for Jesus. Most would agree it is not that serving him is wrong by any means, but that it should not take precedence over "sitting at his feet."

All mean well who preach this message, but I would propose that it has sometimes done unnecessary harm in the Church. Thinking that we are contrasting *being* and *doing*, is it possible that we only have spoken of two kinds of *doing*? The activities may look different outwardly — whether it is prayer or service — but each are still *activities* whether we like to admit it or not. For many people, sitting with Jesus feels more like serving him, and vice versa. Perhaps we felt bad for not serving Jesus enough; now, after hearing about the importance of being with him, we feel bad that we are not spending enough time in prayer. Or perhaps we felt prideful for serving Jesus a lot; now we feel prideful for praying a lot since we have heard that prayer is more important. Maybe we feel ashamed for our inability to strike the perfect balance between *being* and *doing*, or otherwise proud when we get pretty close.

The sad reality is that, for many Christians, all of life has become *doing*, anxiously striving to please the God that is within them. This is what happens when we reduce *being* to a specific kind of action, like prayer. Even prayer becomes a work. The goal here should not be to contrast *being* with *doing*, for in this, we have turned *being* into just one more thing to do. Instead, we should get rid of *doing* altogether and strive only to *be* (in accordance with our new nature) since right doing is a natural result of right being. If we understand our new life in God, then every good activity — including both prayer *and* service — becomes an outflow of our *being* so that there is no more striving, no more works. So once again, the wonderful freedom of the gospel is found first in knowing who and what we are. This is the true meaning of the "rest" for which we are to strive, "for whoever has entered God's rest has also rested from his works..." (Hebrews 4:10).

A friend of mine once admitted that it was hard to comprehend how, in life after death, we would not want to sin anymore. But all one needs to do is to consider how it is that God never sins. It is quite simple — sin is not in his nature (see 1 John 3:5). In other words, God cannot do what God isn't. Or else consider how earthly creatures never sin. From the birds of the air to the fish of the sea, there is no *doing* which conflicts with their true *being*. Just the same, there will be a day when Jesus returns to "transform our lowly body to be like his glorious body" (Philippians 3:21), and we will "become partakers of the divine *nature*" (2 Peter 1:4, my italics), freed forever from the corruption of our flesh which currently wages war against our souls. In the meantime, we must learn to live through Jesus, who has already overcome sin in the flesh and has put on this new nature for us. He is our new *being* (both in person and nature), and we abide in him through faith.

Christ did not die to change our "doing," he died to change our "being." He did not die to redeem our behavior; he died to redeem our nature. He did not die just so that we would love him; he died so that we would become love, as he is love. He did not die for us to remain in the impossibly constant tension between sitting at his feet and serving him; he died so that there would no longer be a distinction between the two. "Whoever abides in me and I in him, he it is that bears much fruit, for apart from me you can do nothing" (John 15:5).

ABIDING IN CHRIST

This is how the Church remains in the sort of works-righteousness mindset that we talked about in the first chapter. We have reduced the things which we already are, by God's doing, into things that we must ourselves do but can never actually accomplish. Take, for example, the idea of "abiding in Christ" (see John 15:1-17). How is it that you have been taught to do this? Personally, I always thought that to abide in Christ, I had to be actively thinking about him, praying, obeying his commands, reflecting on his love for me, etc. How often, then, did I fail to abide in him?! For even when I perceived that I was successful in this matter, it was by my own works, by which no one is united with him. "[R]emember it is not you who support the root, but the root that supports you" (Romans 11:18). The only way one truly abides in the Vine is by trusting that one has already been grafted in through faith. "They were broken off because of their unbelief, but you stand fast through faith" (Romans 11:20). It is not we who connect ourselves to Christ, but Christ who has connected us to himself. By grace alone, "in Christ" is our ongoing state. Therefore, we abide by simply believing it is true.

If you have yet to be convinced, perhaps the Greek will bring the point home. The Greek word translated as "abide" in John 15 is *meno*, which means specifically to "remain" or "stay." This being the case, we might ask, what sense would it make to tell someone to remain where they are not? When someone says they have chosen to *remain* at their job, it is a given that they are speaking of a job they currently have. When a parent tells their child to *stay* at home, we assume that the child is already at home or otherwise will be at home whenever this command becomes relevant. In the same way, Christ's instruction to *remain* or *stay* in him should indicate to believers that we are already there. Christ never commanded us to *get into* him but to stay where he has put us by the same means that we got there — faith.

The same logic applies to many ideas with which we are familiar. For instance, in the same way that we abide in Christ through faith, we "walk by the Spirit" (Galatians 5:16) through faith. There is nothing anyone can do, by an act of their own will, to "get into" the Spirit. As children of God, all believers are in/of the Spirit *by status* or *by nature*. Therefore to *walk* by the Spirit is to live in alignment with our true state of being, which happens naturally when we see ourselves clearly. This is what Paul means when he says, "If we live by the Spirit, let us also keep in step with the Spirit" (Galatians 5:15, cf. 2:20). In other words, he is saying, "Let us act according to who we truly are."

Or how about all this talk of "dying to ourselves?" Have we not yet learned that we are already dead and that Christ is our new life? Once again, there is nothing anyone can do, by an act of their own will, to "die to themselves" except to hand themselves over to Christ, at which point they die completely, immediately, and literally. We *progressively* "die to sin" by considering ourselves *entirely* dead to sin (see Romans 6:11). We crucify the passions of the flesh by believing that "those who belong to Jesus *have crucified* the flesh with its passions and desires" (Galatians 5:24, my italics). We "walk not according to the flesh but according to the Spirit" (Romans 8:4) by believing that we "are not in the flesh but in the Spirit" (Romans 8:9).

If we want to experience the fruit of the Spirit (which can be summed up in *love*), we must stop *trying* to do that which we already *are*, and we must begin to see ourselves as truly one with him. "[T]he love of Christ controls us, because we have concluded this: that one has died for all, therefore all have died" (2 Corinthians 5:14).

I have heard some people screaming since the first chapter, "Grace is not opposed to effort, but to earning!" It is a catchy phrase, but it is not always true. Grace *is* opposed to effort when the effort we put forth is to obtain "the things freely given us by God" (1 Corinthians 2:12) as if we did not already have them, not the least of which is our righteousness and sanctification. Perhaps some think that the way I speak about faith diminishes the responsibility of the believer to respond to God's call with serious personal devotion. But given what I have written thus far, it should be clear that I have no intention to absolve the believer of responsibility for their spiritual growth. On the contrary, my aim is to equip believers with the knowledge of how the gospel actually works to bring about spiritual growth so that there no longer remains an excuse for lukewarm Christianity. To be clear, we should not be opposed to effort (see 2 Peter 1:5-10). But the reader should see by now that effort is a *product* of genuine faith, not the other way around (see 1 Corinthians 15:10). It is not the *means* to obedience; rather, it *is* obedience, which is brought about through faith in Jesus Christ and his finished work. The only striving we must do is the striving to believe, given that we have an adequate understanding of his grace.

Chapter 7

HOW TO BEGIN WALKING BY FAITH

"Rejoice always, pray without ceasing, give thanks in all circumstances; for this is the will of God in Christ Jesus for you" (1 Thessalonians 5:16–18).

I used to read this verse and think, *How in the world is that possible?* It seemed so far from reality that I could hardly even imagine it. Now I know why. It is because I was so frequently walking by sight, a slave to my feelings and circumstances. How could I *genuinely* rejoice when I was feeling everything *but* joy? I was unaware of the permanent unseen reality in which to anchor my soul, let alone how to live there all the time. But the moment that I began striving to believe in the unseen life which Christ had bought for me, I began to see the practicality of these verses. I found myself naturally rejoicing, praying, and giving thanks more often than ever. Whereas it used to seem like an impossibly burdensome commandment, there is now hardly a moment that goes by when I feel it a burden to do these things.

Rather, it is my very lifeline for living and walking in the Spirit. It is the most practical way of thinking that builds my faith, tethers me to the truth, and helps me live free and victorious.

Some will be inclined to call this kind of thinking "denial," and in a way, it is. I take it as a compliment — "If anyone would come after me, let him *deny* himself..." (Matthew 16:24, my italics). When the truth cannot readily be seen or felt, then we must deny that what we see and feel is true. I encourage you to read that sentence one more time. Let us make no mistake about it. If you are in the mind of Christ, you are out of your mind. And there is no better way to live. It is time to start believing in God for what he says — no ifs, ands, or buts about it.

APPLYING IN PRAYER

Since we have spent a lot of time discussing our very real death to sin, let us talk about how we might use prayer to grow in that particular belief and bear the fruit of righteousness.

I am going to assume that you know the importance of acknowledging your sin before God (See Psalm 32 or 1 John 1:5-10). If you have made it this far in the book, then you must care about this. You are under no illusion about your need for his grace. But when you come to God for this purpose, you have essentially two options. One will leave you perpetually waiting on his grace; the other, powerfully walking in it.

The first way of prayer is to ask God for that which we think we do not yet have. Ask him for forgiveness, hoping to persuade him. Ask him for freedom, wondering when he will provide it. Present yourself to him broken and lacking, insisting that he must still do something more to deliver you from your unholy desires and bondage to sin. There is something about this kind of prayer that intuitively may feel more humble and righteous, but it is not grounded in his grace and his promises. When we pray this way, as if we have not fully died to sin, we inevitably either justify our going on in sin or condemn ourselves for still being enslaved to it. This is the antithesis of freedom and victory, stripping faith of all its immediate practical value and turning it into nothing more than hope for the future. But hope is for the future. Faith is for now.

The second, and far better way to pray, I believe, is to praise God and thank him for what he has already given us. We confess our sins, yes, but then we thank him that we are forgiven and cleansed from all unrighteousness (see 1 John 1:9). Rather than begging him to help us further die to ourselves, we rejoice that we have died. Rather than asking that he make us new, we celebrate that he already has. It is not in the slightest bit offensive to God that we so boldly proclaim such things, for they are only true, and not one has been accomplished through a work of our own. Indeed, this is the radical nature of grace, which God had in mind when he sent his Son to save whoever would simply believe. This kind of prayer is how we begin to walk by faith, not by sight.

Not to mention, it appears that this way of thinking and praying is nothing short of a biblical command. As Paul says, "you… *must* consider yourselves dead to sin and alive to God in Christ Jesus" (Romans 6:11, my italics). And "present yourselves to God as those who have been brought from death to life…" (Romans 6:13). What does it say about us if we always come to God broken and empty? This is certainly not the picture of the Christian life put forth in the New Testament. Call it honest if you like, but then you must call God a liar, since according to his gospel, Jesus has made you new and full.

Christians are to "be strong in the Lord and in the strength of his might" (Ephesians 6:10). We are to "lay aside every weight, and sin which clings so closely, and… run with endurance the race that is set before us" (Hebrews 12:1). Yet many Christians have spent their whole lives coming to God as if they are still weak and broken. And every time they ask that he fix them, I imagine him looking down and saying, "What more do you want me to do?" It appears to them that he never answers their prayers, but in reality, they were answered at Calvary.

Now, please understand me. I am not saying there is never a time for a believer to "[b]e wretched and mourn and weep" (James 4:9). When we have veered off course, then godly grief is completely appropriate (see 2 Corinthians 7:10). But let us never mourn in deception, as if we have not already been given everything by God, including new hearts. Let us never believe that we are humbling ourselves before God while refusing to believe his gospel and walk in his grace. To be sure, there is nothing that will keep us more honest and humble, nor that will produce more *godly* grief and repentance than faith in what he has done for us and who we are in him.

On the same note, when we feel troubled, confused, weak, or lost, we *should* cry out to God for help. We do not need to conceal these things from God under a pretense of "faith." *Faith and honesty are never opposed to one another.* In fact, I would argue that being nakedly honest before the Lord is actually a demonstration of our trust in him. That being said, let us make sure that our "honesty" does not actually mean denial of God's word. For instance, you may confide in God that you are feeling wildly anxious and that it is quite a struggle to overcome. It is a fact that you feel this way, and you need not hide it from him (nor *can* you hide it from him). But then you must not stop there, for then you would only be walking by sight, which never produces strength and leaves you enslaved. There is a greater reality which he has given to you, a Spirit he has put inside of you, a life which is hidden in heaven, in which there is no such thing as anxiety. While it is a *fact* that your flesh is feeling anxious, the *truth* is that your spirit is at peace in Jesus. Upon which will you set your mind — facts or truth? According to which will you live — the flesh or the Spirit?

I am also not diminishing the importance of recognizing one's depravity, brokenness, and need for God. To be sure, this is the only kind of soil that is receptive to the seed of the gospel. But once the gospel seed has been effectively planted, "depravity" and "brokenness" are no longer accurate descriptions of the believer. "[Y]ou have been born again, not of perishable seed but of imperishable, through the living and abiding word of God... And this word is the good news that was preached to you" (1 Peter 1:23-25). The kind of prayer where we present ourselves to God as broken sinners is only appropriate until the point that one is delivered from such a state, which is at the moment of belief in Jesus Christ. While we must still acknowledge our sin, we know that it is no longer due to brokenness but deception. Hence the need to start believing in the truth.

Once, we were broken, but now, we are a new creation. Do we think that somehow our newness is still broken, or do we believe that God has fixed the problem? God removed our old hearts and gave us a new one (see Ezekiel 36:26). Was this heart surgery a hack job? Is there something he missed? Or is the heart that he gave us as pure and wonderful as he would want it to be?

You might also think of it this way. We used to be in desperate need of God, in the sense that we did not have him. And while we will always continue to need him, we do not need him in the same sense, for we now have him. A believer's desperate plea for God's presence in their life is a clear sign that they are living out of their feelings, not the gospel truth. For Jesus promised, "I am with you always, to the end of the age" (Matthew 28:20). It is now only appropriate to say, "Lord, I need you" in the context of knowing, "Lord, I have you." It is only appropriate to say, "Lord, do it" in the context of knowing that the Lord has done it. And, oh, what joy this brings! Try it now.

Let us never again think that we need to wait on his grace for freedom and sanctification. His word says that "[h]is divine power *has granted* to us all things that pertain to life and godliness" (2 Peter 1:3, my italics). We have all that we need for life and godliness, so if we lack anything at all in this regard, let us first assume that we lack faith, not grace. If we are to ask God for help, let us ask him for *help to believe* in the good news. If we are to strive for anything, let us strive to believe in the finished work of Jesus Christ. There is no shame at all in saying, "Lord, I believe; help me with my unbelief!" (see Mark 9:24). It may even be that, for the first time in a while, we will actually be praying a prayer that he can answer.

MY BESETTING SIN

For a long time in my life (on and off for 15 years), I wrestled with a pornography addiction. "Addiction" may be too strong of a word, depending on how exactly one thinks of it, but it is appropriate here in the sense that it describes how I could not always control myself. It was what I would call my "besetting sin." It felt like I had tried nearly everything to be free of it — prayer, confession, repentance, accountability partners, accountability software, etc. I truly wanted to be free; I despised this sin (remember Romans 7?). But it seemed like no matter how hard I tried, even if I was able to keep it at bay for weeks or months at a time, I always fell back into it. And even when I was temporarily "clean," there was still a constant battle with lust going on in my mind. The best anyone could tell me was to try harder or to stop trying so hard. The former never worked, and the latter did not sit well with me.

I had been desperate for a solution for years, and one day, I came across a simple practice that would change me forever. It was a wonderful little trick for building faith and praying more effectively. It goes like this. When you ask the Lord for something, only say "please" once. Then, as you continue praying, start saying, "thank you." It may sound a little presumptuous, or perhaps too bold, but it is grounded in an amazing biblical promise: "ask, and it will be given to you; seek, and you will find; knock, and it will be opened to you" (Luke 11:9). And, "whatever you ask in prayer, believe that you have received it, and it will be yours" (Mark 11:24). And, "If you ask me anything in my name, I will do it" (John 14:14). Etc. Saying "thank you" is a simple way of putting your faith into practice. It exposes within your own heart how much you actually believe the Lord will answer you, and thus, provides a sort of benchmark to see if your faith is growing each time you pray. Most importantly, it trains the mind to trust in the Lord — his word, his promises, his provision, his love, his goodness, etc. — despite everything else that tells us to think otherwise.

Some are opposed to this kind of prayer, but it should be quite evident that their contention is with Jesus, not me. I am simply taking God at his word. Perhaps they think it misleads people to pray for things that may not be in God's will. Yet I would propose that there are some things which we can be confident, if not entirely certain, that are always within God's will. We ought to pray for these things boldly and expectantly. One of these things is freedom from sin, which happened to be the content of my prayer, anyway.

When I learned of this new way of praying, I immediately applied it to my addiction. One day, for probably the ten-thousandth time, I prayed, "Lord, will you please free me from pornography forever?" And then it struck me — *I would never again ask God to free me from this addiction.* I would only thank him for having done it. Committed to this new prayer of faith, I said for the first time ever, "Thank you," trying my best to believe that my request had been fulfilled in that very moment. Moving forward, whenever I prayed about this subject, I resolved only to say "thank you," giving praise to God for his perfect deliverance and my total victory, whether I entirely believed it was true or not.[17]

---

[17] This may be obvious, but when I say that I resolved only to say, "thank you," I do not mean that I limited my prayer to literally just those two words. I mean that the content of my prayer was general thanksgiving and praise, with the disposition of believing that I had received what I had asked for. This is in contrast to the way I had prayed in the past, continuing

To my delight, it did not take long for me to actually start believing that God had set me free, the fruit of which was real freedom. Without even knowing it, I was beginning to walk in the power of the gospel and the victory which had been mine all along. I was thanking God for answering my prayer that day, and I was learning to walk in the belief that he had delivered me. But what I had yet to perceive is that my newfound freedom from pornography was not so much an answer to prayer as it was the result of my faith. Nor was it a special outpouring of grace, but rather, an application of the truth which is true of every Christian the moment they are born again.

Within a week or two of praying this way, I had a dream, which I think drives this point home very nicely. It was the type that is so vivid and peculiar that, upon awaking, one immediately suspects is from God.

A DREAM ANALOGY

In my dream, I was being watched and followed by some sort of mafia. There was a bounty on my head, and everywhere I went, I saw these threatening characters standing in the distance. I was fearful, anxious, and constantly wondering when they were going to "get" me.

> "For evils have encompassed me beyond number; my iniquities have overtaken me, and I cannot see; they are more than the hairs of my head; my heart fails me" (Psalm 40:12).

---

to ask for it as if God had not yet answered, waiting for explicit evidence to confirm otherwise.

After much of this torment, there was a great turning point in the dream when I walked into their meeting house unannounced. I went straight up to the mob boss, who just happened to be sitting at a round table playing poker with his associates. I tapped him on the shoulder, and when he spun his head around, I handed him my father's credit card, which contained an endless supply of money — as much as he would ever need and more — to remove my apparent debt. (I guess I had a rich Father.) The bounty was removed from my head, and I walked out of that house a free man.

> "[He canceled] the record of debt that stood against us with its legal demands. This he set aside, nailing it to the cross. He disarmed the rulers and authorities and put them to open shame, by triumphing over them in [Jesus]" (Colossians 2:14-15).

Already, I would say it was a pretty cool dream, but here is where it gets especially interesting.

Later in the dream, as I was enjoying my new life of freedom, I heard a knock on the door. To my surprise, when I opened it, I saw *me*. But the person was not exactly like me — he was anxious, frightened, and wearied. He told me that he was in danger and that I was, too. There were people after him, and he was convinced that I must go with him and run to stay safe. I quickly realized that he was me *from before the incident*.

My response to him was casual and dismissive. I was not the least bit persuaded to go with him (although I did feel some pity for the poor soul), for I knew beyond a shadow of a doubt that he was *no longer I*. There was no question about it, no reason to ponder. I was there when my debt was paid. He could not convince me otherwise.

"Get out of here," I said as I shut the door in his face and moved on with my new life. Before the dream was over, this encounter happened a couple more times in the very same way.

> "For freedom Christ has set us free; stand firm therefore, and do not submit again to a yoke of slavery" (Galatians 5:1).

When I awoke, I knew that God was trying to tell me something very important, and in the coming months, its meaning and application became more clear and more powerful to me as he revealed through Scripture what he had done for me in Christ. Here is my basic interpretation.

The crux of the dream was the incident when I paid off the mob boss with my Father's credit card, which clearly symbolizes Jesus' death on the cross and payment for my sins. Therefore, the first part of the dream, prior to that event, represented my slavery to sin and the power of evil over me. This was my life before Jesus. And the freedom I experienced later in the dream seemed related to the freedom I had begun to experience regarding my addiction to pornography, and actually, freedom from sin in general. This being the case, what immediately caught my attention is the means by which I became free. It was through the payment of my debt (i.e. Jesus' death) and nothing else. It was as if the Lord was telling me that the freedom I had recently prayed for regarding my addiction to pornography had been accomplished long before I ever prayed for it — not as a result of prayer, but through the finished work of

Christ. I had simply not been walking in that grace until I began praying and believing that it was there.

Even more fascinating to me is the part of the dream when my old self came back into the picture, convinced that I was still under oppression and needed to go with him. No matter what he said, I simply knew that it was not true. Due to the earlier (Cross) event, I was confident in my new freedom, and I had no reason to follow him. This is powerful.

In my own life up to that point, I realized that the reason I had kept falling back into this sin was not due to a lack of deliverance but a lack of accurate belief. I was only enslaved to sin (although not really) because I *believed* I was. Every time the old man (the flesh) came around — say, with an impure thought or powerful feeling — trying to convince me that I was not entirely free, I simply went along with him as if it were true, trying to keep from sinning by my own strength, and weighed down by the seeming inevitability of failure. Then when I failed, it reinforced the belief that I was still under the power of sin, and I continued living under oppression. Sound familiar to anyone?

In my mind, I thought that I needed hard evidence before I could claim total freedom. In other words, I was always looking to string together months or years of purity to prove that I had overcome this sin. But of course, this is actually the very mindset that kept me imprisoned for so long. The solution? Look only to the cross. The moment that I found confidence in my victory through the finished work of Christ, rather than anything else, is the moment that sin stopped being able to control me.

In the months after this revelation, there were but a couple of final times when I fell back into that sin (or relapsed). But these instances were not like the rest, for one reason. Afterward, I did not let the sin convince me that I was not yet victorious. Instead, I simply realized that I had been duped. My flesh came knocking at the door, and I momentarily believed the lie that he was still me. Once I came to my senses, all I needed to do was look back to the cross to confirm the truth, walking out of it once again a perfectly free man, giving thanks to God through Jesus Christ that I had been made new.

In all honesty, this was not as easy to do as it is to retell. Believing in the face of lies takes conviction, trust, persistence, and effort. But the effort is in believing and walking in what God says is true, rather than striving to make something true which is yet to be. The two are very different.

The flesh (and Satan) will come on strong at times, making a superbly convincing case that we are still in sin, that we have not yet been made new. But we need only to look to the cross to see that through Jesus, we have died to sin and that the voice of the flesh is no longer who we are. We may say to ourselves, "If I am truly free, then why am I being bombarded with all these fleshy thoughts and feelings?" We may be tempted to think that because there is an ongoing battle, there is not yet perfect freedom. But then we have misunderstood the battle. Our *freedom* has been won; we must now fight to *believe*. Our *freedom* is perfect; our *faith* is not. We must now "[look] to Jesus, the founder and perfecter of our faith" (Hebrews 12:2).

We might even find that in moments (or even seasons) of weakness, we have fallen into the trap, believed the lie, followed the flesh, and given into temptations of all sorts. Does this mean that we are still our same old selves, in the flesh and sold under sin? By no means! Does this nullify the grace and faithfulness of God or undo the work of Christ, which is received through faith alone? Absolutely not! It means we were lied to; we were gullible; and it is time now to plant ourselves firmly in the unchanging truth of the gospel, as opposed to the always-changing state of the flesh. It is time to "put off your old [man], which belongs to your former manner of life and is corrupt through deceitful desires, and... be renewed in the spirit of your minds, and... put on the new [man], created after the likeness of God in true righteousness and holiness" (Ephesians 4:22-24). This is true repentance — putting off falsehood and putting on Truth; believing in the unseen reality, despite what we see.

A BREAKTHROUGH IN PRAYER

One morning as I was spending time in prayer, my wife came into the room and sat down to do the same. As I was finishing up my prayers, I felt an unusual urge to pray over her, although I did not know why. So I offered to lay my hands on her to do so, and she accepted my offer. At one point, while I was praying over her, I had a strong sense of God's presence over the both of us. It was really a wonderful feeling! I gave voice to this by saying to my wife, "Wow, do you feel that?!" I do not believe she responded at the moment, but I did not think anything of it. Having believed that I had kicked her day off with a good, husbandly blessing, I finished my prayer, left the room, and went about my day.

Little did I know, she had woken up that morning feeling unusually far from God. Inwardly, she was feeling weak and weighed down by his apparent absence. So when I reveled in his presence and asked if she could feel it, too, I only made matters far worse because she did not feel a thing! Immediately, this made her wonder what was wrong with her since she could not feel what I felt. And it reaffirmed her suspicion that God was not with her. How horrible a feeling, but how wonderful an opportunity! For there is no better time to grow in one's faith than when we cannot *see* or *feel* what God's word says is true.

To my wife's credit, this is not the end of the story. At that point in our lives, we had just begun learning about how to walk in faith. And after I left the room, when she was alone with God, she had a decision to make. Was she going to allow her feelings to dictate her beliefs, or would she fight to believe what God's word clearly says is true? Was she going to give in to this despair, wonder why God was not with her, and begrudgingly go about her day "without" him? Or was she going to renounce her reliance on the flesh and rejoice in the reality of his presence and fullness in her life?

That day, she chose the latter of the two. She thanked God for his perfect presence, for never leaving her, and always being close, even though she did not feel it. She praised him for making her new and fully pleasing to him, despite her feelings of shame and unworthiness. She chose not to focus on how she felt but instead to focus on God's word. Worth noting is that she did not have to *pretend* that she felt differently. She could acknowledge how she felt while at the same time recognizing the irrelevance of her feelings and proclaiming the truth over her life. It was short and simple, but it was powerful. Within ten or fifteen minutes, she felt as close to God as ever, and she learned firsthand the power of faith to overcome the flesh.

How easily she could have succumbed to her feelings, believing the lies of the enemy who so manipulates the flesh. It is not hard to imagine how she might have reached out to her Christian friends that day, asking them to pray for her spiritual state as if there were no other recourse besides prayer and waiting. And worse, who knows how long this spiritual stupor could have continued as she waited on God to answer her prayer. Days turn into weeks, and weeks turn into months. Before long, she determines she is in a "dry season," even longer, and she is in a "spiritual desert" — blindly standing at the eternal wellspring of life, yet waiting for God to provide refreshment. And if ever she did start to *feel* better about things, she would be as much a slave to her flesh as ever before, still rising and falling with the fickleness of feelings, making Satan's job easy as he plays her like a fiddle. No doubt, she would have remained in spiritual infancy, never having found her way to "the pure spiritual milk" (1 Peter 2:2) by which one grows.

To me, this story highlights in a very simple way how one begins to walk in faith and overcome. It really is this simple. There is no promise that it will be easy — in fact, quite the opposite. But every effort we make to believe in the face of lies will result in strength and sanctification that we could never have obtained otherwise.

You might now be wondering, "How often do I do this? Am I just supposed to be rejoicing and giving thanks all the time?" And in response, I would lead you back to the scripture that was quoted at the beginning of the chapter.

"Rejoice always, pray without ceasing, give thanks in all circumstances; for this is the will of God in Christ Jesus for you" (1 Thessalonians 5:16–18).

I have found no better way to remain grounded in unseen truth than this. If you want to be established in the faith, then abound in thanksgiving for every promise, every gift, every truth, and every command in Scripture (see Colossians 2:6-7).

Chapter 8

HOW THE GOSPEL
APPLIES TO EVERYTHING

Hopefully, you see by now that faith is much more than attending to our churchly duties, having peace through difficult circumstances, having the assurance of our salvation, or even taking occasional bold risks for the kingdom. These are certainly part of it, but truth is applicable in literally every moment of the day, which means that faith is applicable just as often. As cliché as it may sound, Jesus really is always the answer. The gospel applies to every area of our lives, leaving nothing untouched by the power of the Cross and Resurrection.

In this chapter, I hope to show you in a wide variety of ways how this is true. Taking all that we have learned so far, we will use some examples of day-to-day struggles that are relatable and common among us to demonstrate how it is that we can begin to stand in the truth and overcome.

"For everyone who has been born of God overcomes the world. And this is the victory that has overcome the world—our faith" (1 John 5:4).

UNFORGIVENESS

"For if you forgive others their trespasses, your heavenly Father will also forgive you, but if you do not forgive others their trespasses, neither will your Father forgive your trespasses" (Matthew 6:14–15).

We do not like to acknowledge this verse (and others like it), but it is there nonetheless. Let no one fool you into thinking that God forgives your sins if you are still willfully holding onto bitterness or resentment in your heart toward others. God, himself, says otherwise. Do not reason your way out of the plain meaning of his word. Instead, give thanks that God has shared his forgiving heart with you, for his word is now in you. If there is even one person whom you refuse to forgive, just one whom you fail to extend the same grace that God has given you in Christ Jesus, then you are rejecting the grace that God has shown you.

> *How can this be so? Are we not saved by grace alone through faith alone? Are you saying that forgiveness is work that I must do to be saved?*

Forgiveness is not something you must do to be forgiven. It is *evidence* that the truth is in you — the Truth being Jesus, who died for *all*. "[W]hoever lacks [it] is so nearsighted that he is blind, having forgotten that he was cleansed from his former sins" (2 Peter 1:9). Remember that you "have been crucified with Christ" (Galatians 2:20), and now the crucified Christ is your life and identity. If you believe this truth and live according to his Spirit within you, then you will see others from this perspective, and you will give your life for them as Jesus did. It is not simply what you need to do, despite what you want. It is who you are and what you want to do, despite what you feel.

This may seem like a hard word, but please do not be deceived. A hard word is one that leaves you with a hard heart, defined by what others have done to you rather than who Jesus is in you. I am truly sorry that you have been hurt. This was never the way that it was supposed to be. God hates injustice, and he weeps with you. He does not make light of your pain and suffering. Rather, he is the most compassionate being in existence — so much so that he stopped at nothing to make up for what has been done to you. The Father did not give up his Son in order to simply acknowledge and relate to your pain. He gave up his Son to heal you and make you strong. Christ is a victor; therefore, the one who is in him is not a victim. You have been vindicated; therefore, you have no need to be validated. Renounce the lie, and believe the truth.

But I am a good Christian otherwise. Doesn't that count for anything?

There is no amount of obedience in the world that can make up for a lack of mercy. In Matthew 9:13, Jesus tells the Pharisees, "Go and learn what this means: 'I desire mercy, and not sacrifice.' For I came not to call the righteous, but sinners." God desires mercy; therefore, you do, too.

But they were in the wrong, and they treated me unjustly.

And while hanging on the Cross, Jesus cried, "Father, forgive them, for they know not what they do" (Luke 23:34). Put on the mind of Christ, and you will see that this complaint is not from him. You now have a new purpose, and it is to shine *his* light, manifest *his* life, and complete *his* sufferings. Rejoice in this, for it is the very reason you exist, and it is where you will find true freedom.

I cannot or do not want to let go of it.

That is your flesh speaking, or else it is Satan. The Spirit within you — who is your life and identity — is already free of it. He loves this person. He gave his life for this person. He *is* love, and as such, he does not keep a record of wrongdoing (see 1 Corinthians 13:5). He gladly "bears all things, believes all things, hopes all things, endures all things" (1 Corinthians 13:7). And he is in you; therefore, you do, too. Unforgiveness is deception. Tell God, "Thank you for giving me your heart for this person."

I am trying to let go of it, but it is proving to be very difficult. I still feel very angry.

Praise God that your spirit is willing! Be encouraged that you are fighting. It is hard for you to see now, but you already have let go of it (in spirit). The anger that you continue to feel is of the flesh and from the enemy. Do not be deceived into believing that you still carry resentment or hurt. You may very well feel it, and you can be honest about your feelings before God. But if you believe that they are from *you*, rather than your flesh, you will lose the battle. Since feelings no longer dictate your beliefs, you are free to believe that you have forgiven. Abide in the truth. Abide in Christ. Continue thanking God that he has poured his overwhelming love for this person into your heart —

because he has (see Romans 5:5) — and walk according to that reality. As you do, your spirit will become stronger, and you will bear the fruit of his love, which has been there since you first believed.

SLOTH

Let's say that you are tempted with the desire to watch television instead of spending your time more productively as you know you should. In the past, you would have taken the temptation to mean that there is apparently still some laziness to root out of your heart. You would have thought, if you just loved God more, this would not be a problem. You would have felt like you truly *wanted* to indulge in television, despite feeling that you should not. The ultimate conclusion would be that your will is not in alignment with God's. You are lazy, you are a sinner, and you still have some "dying" to do.

All of these thoughts occur within a split second, of course, and by that point, before you had even decided what to do, you had already lost. Whether or not you decided to indulge in television in that moment, you believed the lie that you wanted to. You identified with the flesh, thinking that its desires were your own. Therefore you gained no ground in terms of gospel freedom, for your understanding of self did not come into further alignment with the truth.

That is how you used to handle such encounters with laziness. But now it is different because you know who you are. In the same scenario, you hear the voice saying, "It sounds nice to be lazy, doesn't it?" You feel the burning desire to agree, the flesh raging to get its fix. Everything in you says, "I want this, I want this!" except the Word of God, who says, "No, you do not." Then you look to Christ and his glory, and you recognize that because these feelings cannot be his, neither are they your own. They come entirely from the flesh, which is *on* you, not *in* you. They are like a cancer on the skin, as opposed to a cancer in the soul. It is not a product of *you*; it is a foreign entity on you, causing you some temporary discomfort. There is no defilement of thought because it is not your thought. There is no unholiness of desire because they are not your desires. There is no fault in you whatsoever because you are not even in the flesh (see Romans 8:9).

So how do you approach the throne with this temptation to be lazy? You give thanks to God for making you clean and holy. You thank him that you do not want to be lazy at all and that you love being productive and prayerful! You do not *feel* it in the moment. In fact, you feel exactly the opposite. But you no longer walk by feelings. You walk by faith in God's word. And you rejoice that he has given you *his* energy and diligence, making you new in *his* image.

ANGER

I was speaking with a pastor-friend once who told me that he had always thought of himself as an angry person. This self-assessment only seemed accurate in his eyes, given how constantly he felt anger boiling beneath the surface. This had become a part of his identity, and therefore, a seemingly inescapable reality. Knowing he was a believer, I looked him in the eyes and said, "Brother, you are not an angry person." Tears filled his eyes as he had never considered that to be a possibility. How could I be so certain? Because God's word says so. By definition of being in Christ, the flesh is no longer is an accurate expression of him. Christ is his life and identity, and Christ is the most gentle and patient person the world has ever known. "[W]e regard no one according to the flesh... if anyone is in Christ, he is a new creation" (2 Corinthians 5:16-17). My friend was only seeing himself wrongly, and therefore, experienced lifelong slavery to this false self-image.

Not surprisingly, he immediately questioned why it was, then, that he always felt anger and why he was so often unable to control it. I told him that the true culprit of his anger was his own body of flesh, rather than his spirit, and he had just not yet learned how to live by faith according to the Spirit within him. Within just a few short days of walking by faith in his newness, he began to experience freedom from anger that he had never felt before.

COMMUNING WITH GOD

One day recently, I was driving in the car alone for about an hour and a half. I am not exaggerating when I say that I was in a state of euphoria for most of the trip, an unbroken smile stretching from ear to ear. I was not just in a good mood that day. Nor was this due to beautiful weather or the right music or any other sort of temporal thing. Rather, I was just being with God in silence, basking in his perfect love and reciprocating it in a measure that I never thought possible. What made this time of communion so overwhelmingly sweet is that I believed more than ever that *my love for God* was as pure and undefiled as *his love for me*. It was *mutually* fulfilling in a way I had never experienced. And most importantly, it was driven by faith, not just fleshy feelings.

At one point, the thought came into my mind that perhaps I was not being sincere, that I did not truly love God like I was "pretending" to love him in this moment. In the past, this may have led me down a rabbit trail of doubt, ultimately stealing from this wonderfully intimate moment. But *because I was grounded in the truth*, the thought went away as soon as it came, and my communion with God remained uninterrupted. The Bible says that God's own love, which is perfect, is in my heart (see Romans 5:5). Therefore the gospel gave me permission, or rather, it required me to believe that this self-deprecating thought could not be true. In other words, the truth defended me in this time of communion so that the enemy could not step in and ruin it with his lies.

In prayer, we must be able to say to God, "I love you with all of my heart." And we must not doubt that this love is sincere. When experiencing intimacy with God, the enemy will attempt to disrupt. He may assault you with evil thoughts, making you feel defiled, unrighteous, or unworthy. Do not be surprised if, in the midst of enjoying God, you hear things like: *This isn't real. You don't actually love God like this. Who are you kidding? You aren't being sincere. You'd rather be doing something else. Look at how you sinned just earlier today. Do you really think God is pleased with you? Do you really think he enjoys you?*

But if you become fortified in the truth, you will find that the truth defends you so that these types of thoughts can no longer distract you or affect you at all. In this way, unwavering faith leads to unbroken communion.

ADDICTION

Many recovery programs for addicts embrace the motto of "once an addict, always an addict." They worry that if a person believes he is no longer an addict, then he will be more liable to getting caught off guard when temptations arise, and therefore, more vulnerable to relapse. This may be true for an unbeliever who has not been transformed by Jesus. But the gospel leaves no room whatsoever for this insidious mindset. "[I]f anyone is in Christ, he is a new creation. The old has passed away; behold, the new has come" (2 Corinthians 5:17). If one never wavers in this belief, then it will be impossible to relapse. This is not to say that one cannot again be tempted. We should not be the least bit surprised when temptations come. But now we are armed when temptations come because we know where they come from — the flesh, not the spirit. Therefore we are not deceived when they arise, and we are equipped to battle the lie with the truth. Repentance, accountability, and support are all helpful and important. But the truth of the gospel will set you free as nothing else can.

SEXUALITY

There is quite a lot of confusion today, even in the Church, regarding matters of human sexuality. But when we see the gospel clearly, it sheds much light on the matter. As we have said, the grace of God is much more than forgiveness and a ticket to heaven. It powerfully delivers us from the sinful passions of the flesh and makes us one with Christ. Therefore, after hearing the truth about the gospel, to continue living according to the flesh — identifying with it rather than with Christ — is to reject the grace of God and prove that one's faith is not genuine.

One who identifies as a homosexual, for instance, is not identifying with Christ. To be sure, this is true for every form of sin. "God is light, and in him is no darkness at all" (1 John 1:5). As with any other desire of the flesh, whether or not a person experiences homosexual attraction has no bearing on what is true of their spirit. A person's sexuality is entirely a matter of the flesh, not of the spirit. We could also say the same about one's gender, for "there is no male and female… in Christ Jesus" (Galatians 3:28). While the reality of the flesh is there, it does not define who we are or what we really want, nor does it give us a license to sin. If we believe it does, then we have misunderstood the gospel, which says we have died to sin and put off the flesh.

Frankly, it does not matter what a person was born into if that person has died and been born *again*. Every person on earth was born into a body of flesh with sinful passions. Yet "those who belong to Christ Jesus have crucified the flesh with its passions and desires" (Galatians 5:24). If you have been born again in Christ, then you have been "created after the likeness of God in true righteousness and holiness" (Ephesians 4:24). Everything else is falsehood. Put it off and walk in the truth. You are no longer in/of the flesh. If you live according to it, you will die in your sins, but if you live according to the Spirit within you, you will have life abundantly. "For to set the mind on the flesh is death, but to set the mind on the Spirit is life and peace" (Romans 8:6).

There is plenty more to say on this topic, but rather than address all the different angles of it, I will simply say this as an encouragement to the Church. Seek first to understand the gospel, and everything else will become clear.

BY HIS WOUNDS, WE ARE HEALED

There are some things which, for one reason or another, many Christians believe have no gospel solution. Maybe they do not believe this *technically*, but practically. In other words, they believe that God *can* do it — on the sole basis that he is all-powerful — but not really that he *will* do it, let alone that he already has. I am thinking of things like anxiety, depression, addiction, eating disorders, emotional trauma, ADHD, etc. What all these have in common is that, in many cases, we may not describe them as *sin* but as *sickness* or *corruption*. The diagnoses involve a problem within the body (usually the brain), rather than the soul.

I think most Christians would agree that the gospel should deliver us from sin, but there is much less agreement about its healing effect on the body. Hence why, even in the Church, the default treatment for such things is often counseling, medication, support groups, and so on. There is nothing inherently wrong with these other forms of treatment; they can even be quite helpful. And to the extent that it is God's will for you to be well — which I believe it generally is — then you should seek wellness however it may come. That being said, I believe wholeheartedly that there is a more powerful and holistic solution to such conditions — that is, *persevering faith* in the finished work of Christ.

To be clear, I am not providing medical advice here. I speak as a pastor, a spiritual guide, not a health professional. I have no intention of replacing anyone's doctor or counselor, nor to convince anyone to discontinue the kinds of treatments aforementioned. They have their place and can be a great blessing. As a minister of the word, I specialize in the gospel and nothing else. Therefore, I cannot, with integrity, offer advice regarding other forms of treatment, positively or negatively. I only intend to show you that the gospel is more relevant, and faith more practical, than you may have thought.

To make my case, let us use depression as an example. Perhaps your psychiatrist has determined that it is a chemical imbalance in the brain. Or perhaps there are circumstantial reasons that you attribute to your condition. Whatever the reason, it is imperative you realize — if you are a believer — that the depression is not in your heart/spirit but in your flesh. In other words, you must make the distinction that it is not in *you* but in your body. How can you be so sure? Because the fruit of the Spirit is joy! Through faith in Jesus, you have been made one with the Spirit of Joy who lives in you. Can the Spirit of God be depressed (or anxious, unfocused, addicted, restless, traumatized, etc.)? Most certainly not! So, *as a matter of fact*, neither are you (in spirit). Remember, Christ is your new life and identity. Therefore you cannot at the same time identify with depression while also identifying with Christ, in whom there is no depression. To do so is deception.

Please hear me. This does not in any way diminish the fact that you are really experiencing depression, nor is it to suggest that you should just get over it quite easily. Rather, it is to clarify what the *source* is so that you know how to fight back. You may feel it, sure, but you must not *identify* with it, as if it is in your spirit. When feeling depressed, it is most natural to think to yourself, "*I* am depressed." But this is the lie that Satan loves for you to believe. The truth is that your *flesh* is manifesting depression, and it is waging war against your *spirit*, which is not yet strong and mature. You do not need more joy and contentment. You already have it by the Spirit of God within you. You now need to abide in him by believing it is so, putting off the lie that the flesh is an expression of *you*. Once again, this is very different from trying to make yourself joyful or pretending that you are. Faith is not striving to become something you are not. It is striving to believe that you already are what God says you are. Moreover, faith is not pretending or mere positive thinking. It is a *conviction* of truth that you cannot currently see (see Hebrews 11:1).

There is one thing that defines you now — Christ in you. Relentlessly thank God that he has delivered you from relying on your flesh and your feelings for happiness. You are learning to experience joy *through* him. Rejoice that he has given you joy inexpressible, and renounce every lie that says otherwise. You can even rejoice as you suffer through this because it gives you the opportunity to put off the flesh and grow strong in spirit (see Romans 5:3-5). Then, have great hope in the fact that as you become more grounded in the truth, the Spirit within you will begin to give life to your mortal flesh, putting to death the depression within the body so that it no longer is able to wage war against you at all (see Romans 8:10-13). There is no corruption in the Vine; therefore, corruption will not remain in its abiding branches.

You could certainly pray that God would just remove the depression from your body. And perhaps he would; perhaps he would not. Either way, this leaves you waiting and powerless until God decides to act. Moreover, it leaves you relying on the flesh to be free from depression instead of relying on the Spirit to be free from the flesh. So the better option, I believe, is to take hold of the grace you have been given.[18] Strive to believe in the unseen reality in which the Bible says you live, where there is not even such a thing as depression.

If you want to take it a step further, ask God to help you identify whatever lies are afflicting you. Then fight back with the truth. Do you feel as if your life, or certain aspects of it, are meaningless? Is there too much weight and responsibility on your shoulders to handle? Are there people you have not forgiven, hurts that have not healed, dreams you have failed to attain, regrets you have been unable to let go of? Whatever it is, diligently seek what God's word says about it, and then prayerfully strive to believe his word, giving thanks and putting on Christ by faith. Do this with each and every lie that comes to the surface, and do it until it is gone. As you grow stronger in faith, living increasingly according to the Spirit, your joy will come from heaven, and nothing will be able to take it from you.

Another thought that you may be oppressed with is that you do not even *want* to be full of joy, that there is some sick and twisted reason you prefer depression over freedom. Notice how this degrades your spirit, so you must know that it also is a lie. "[T]he desires of the flesh are against the Spirit... to keep you from doing the things *you want to do*" (Galatians 5:17, my italics). What this scripture implies is that you truly desire what the Spirit of God within you desires, and this is *always* freedom. No matter how strongly you feel a given desire is your own, if it is opposed to the desires of the Spirit (i.e. the will of God), then it is

---

[18] I might add that there is no reason you cannot do this alongside medication and/or counseling.

from your flesh, not from you. Do not be deceived. Again, thank God that he has given you all of *his* desires, despite what you feel in a given moment.

Now, if you understand what I have said about depression, then it should be quite easy to see how it applies to other things, as well — emotional trauma, addiction, ADHD, anxiety, sleeplessness, etc. If it does not describe Jesus, then it no longer describes you. A great mantra to hold for such things as these is this: "By his wounds you have been healed" (1 Peter 2:24). God says it is so. Will you humbly receive his word, despite what you currently feel? Like so many amazing aspects of the gospel, this is an *unseen* truth that will only become visible by believing it.

These conditions we have mentioned are conditions *of the flesh*, with which we no longer identify since we now live by the Spirit. To identify as an addict, to identify with old wounds, or to identify with the corruption of the flesh at all — as if they define who you are — is to undermine the power of the Cross and the Resurrection by which you have been united with Christ. You put off the flesh and been born again to new life (see Colossians 2:11-12), with God's character and incorruptible nature. This life may be hidden (see Colossians 3:3), but it is nonetheless real. Take hold of it by faith, and never look back.

THE BATTLE

In the case that you have not yet discovered this for yourself, we might as well acknowledge it here. Walking by faith is not always a walk in the park. It is truly the "narrow gate" that few will find (see Matthew 7:13-14). As you begin to exercise your faith, you may notice how quickly you are confronted or even assaulted with conflicting thoughts, feelings, and trials of various kinds. You will begin to see how all of life is a spiritual war zone and how every waking moment is an opportunity to become stronger and prevail. This may sound burdensome at first, but actually, faith is the only thing that brings us into genuine rest from our works (see Matthew 11:28-30). And we need not wait for that rest to come. It can be found at all times in the hidden life with Christ in heaven. As we grow in faith, living more through Christ, we become much less like battle-weary soldiers hanging onto life by a thread and more like battle-hungry, blood-bathed conquerors charging forward in the strength of the LORD. The armor may initially seem like an awkward fit, but soon you will become very comfortable in it (see Ephesians 6:10-18).

As you transform your way of thinking, praying, and proclaiming these unseen truths over your life, the first thing you might notice is a feeling of dishonesty. It may feel a bit disingenuous to tell God "thank you" for something you do not yet see or feel. This is actually not a bad thing. The feelings of dishonesty just mean that you are finally confronting your unbelief head-on. It is far worse to go your whole life thinking that your faith is strong and genuine, only to remain in spiritual infancy for the length of your days. Just remember, when your doubts and fears are exposed, they are only being exposed for the first time *to you*. God knew they were there all along. Now, the false pretense is removed; you and God are on the same page; you have a better idea of how and what to pray. I often say, "Lord, I believe, but help me with my unbelief" (see Mark 9:24).

The next thing that you might notice is that you do not see an immediate transformation. Do not let this discourage you or lead you astray from the truth. The passions of the flesh are like a stray cat. Having habitually fed them your whole life, you should not be surprised when they do not leave you immediately. It is likely that they will keep returning for a while before they finally realize that it is pointless, and they will leave you for good. Either way, you must never wait for the fruit in order to determine what is true. This is not faith; therefore, it will not produce the results you desire. Regardless of what is occurring in your flesh, relentlessly abide in the truth of Christ and his finished work, and the fruit will inevitably come.

If ever you are struggling to overcome a particular sin, the answer is the same as any other time — *believe*. This is your repentance, for you cannot truly believe and continue in sin (see Romans 6:2). The extent to which you are still overcome by sin is the extent to which you have not yet fully believed the gospel. There is no reason to be ashamed of this. Just recognize that your faith is not yet perfect and continue to grow in it. "[Forget] what lies behind and [strain] forward to what lies ahead" (Philippians 3:13). Worth noting is that, while you may know the gospel intellectually, this does not necessarily mean that you believe it in your heart. The former has very little power compared to the latter. I know intellectually that I am dead to sin, but it is very clear that at times that I do not fully believe it or even fully understand it. So I continue to ask God for a deeper revelation of the truth that I already accept, and he is always faithful to answer that prayer. Remember, *knowledge becomes revelation through prayer.*

The flesh may land some punches, but take heart that the war has already been won. It makes no difference whether you have been caught up in the flesh for a few hours or a few months. The truth of who you are in Christ has not changed. The grace of God compels you to leave the past behind and move forward in truth. I believe that these moments of clarity that follow periods of darkness are actually some of the most opportune times to tackle the lies that have caused you to sin. You may experience sincere, godly grief, but do not waste these moments of clarity by being weighed down with guilt and condemnation or beating yourself up for not having enough faith. Instead of focusing on all the time that you spent being deceived, take advantage of every moment that you have your wits about you, despite how infrequently they seem to come at first. Soon you will find your mind being renewed, and your life transformed. "Do not be conformed to this world, but be transformed by the renewal of your mind..." (Romans 12:2).

Chapter 9

SOME HELPFUL CLARIFICATIONS

Up to this point, we have covered a lot of ground. Let us take a moment to summarize before finishing up.

We have learned that love is not actually the means to obedience like we may have thought. As long as we continue merely relying on our willpower, we are under the law and enslaved to sin. The gospel does far more than motivate the evil heart to do good. God transforms the heart entirely, in an instant, and makes it pure. We no longer need to pray and wait for our love to increase because "God's love has been poured into our hearts through the Holy Spirit who has been given to us" (Romans 5:5). Now that it is there, we must believe that it is there, despite what is occurring in our flesh that might say otherwise. This is how "faith work[s] through love" (Galatians 5:6). We do not necessarily need deeper repentance; we need deeper faith. We might now say that to repent *is* to believe. When we have a correct understanding of God's grace and the love within us, faith propels us out of sin, unlike anything else.

Our flesh is now the source of all our sinful passions. This is not at all to say that our flesh is evil; rather, it is the *desires* of the flesh that are manipulated by evil in order to deceive our spirits into sin. Moreover, the flesh is not a sinful *spirit*, or an old *self*, or a false *self*. It is not to be confused with the self/spirit at all. We are not our flesh, rather, we are *in* a body of flesh. And we overcome its sinful passions — making and keeping it holy — not by striving to obey God out of our own willpower, but by *identifying* with Christ alone, i.e. walking according to the Spirit. In the flesh, the law tells us *what to do*. In the Spirit, the law tells us *who we are*. Thus, to walk in the flesh is to simply do our best to obey God's word, but to walk in the Spirit is to believe that the Word is our new life and identity.

Moreover — since we were baptized into Christ — just as Christ is in us, we are in him. Because Christ was crucified in the flesh and raised in the spirit, we too have a new and unseen life that is not in the flesh but in the spirit with Christ in heaven. By faith, therefore, we are no longer captive to the sin and corruption of the flesh. We have died to the flesh and been born again to God. We are not even of this world anymore but of heaven. We share in God's nature, having become his children. Although this is not complete — since we have not ourselves been resurrected bodily — the Spirit within us now conveys the power of Jesus' resurrection to our mortal bodies. Our humanity is increasingly redeemed as we abide in him by faith.

All along the way, we must know that we are clean. Jesus did not only die for the forgiveness of our sins, but for the removal of our sin. This work is complete, and it is the very meaning of *atonement*. You are not guilty; you are pure; you are righteous in God's sight. He sees it because it is true, and it is all by his own doing. You have never loved him so much as when you realized how he looks at you and why.

For the believer, guilt, shame, and condemnation are *always* from the devil and *never* from God. Satan is your Accuser. God is your Redeemer.

It is not a cop-out to say that God has removed our sin as if we can somehow go on sinning while believing this is true. On the contrary, it is the only truth that sets us free from sin since our identity drives our actions. Failure to obey him is now a product of unbelief. Thus, we need to renew our minds and grow in faith that we truly are as he says we are — dead to sin. We must rely on his word for truth, not on what we see and feel. And perhaps the best way to begin doing so is by prayers of thanksgiving and rejoicing in the truth.

Having seen now how the gospel applies to a wide variety of scenarios in our lives, I hope you have begun to put what you have learned into practice. My prayer for you is that you begin to have your own inward revelation of these truths, and more, that you do not get discouraged as you fight nor led astray by the lies of the enemy. Seek the Lord in prayer, relying on him to reveal the meaning of the Scriptures to you, and trust that he will lead you into all truth (see John 16:13).

In this next-to-last chapter, we will look at just a few more concepts that I believe will strengthen our foundation and help bring clarity to some unanswered questions.

JESUS WAS TEMPTED

As you battle temptation, it is not uncommon to get discouraged. Satan wants you to feel like you are failing so that you will give up the fight altogether. But as you try to make sense of what is occurring inside of you in these times,

I have found it quite helpful to look at what occurred in Jesus when he was on the earth. The incarnation has much to teach us.

Consider this. How is it that Jesus was "in every respect... tempted as we are, yet without sin" (Hebrews 4:15)? Perhaps the most common answer to this question is simply that he was God. I agree that he was fully God, but this is a very cheap and unthoughtful answer, which fails to acknowledge also the fullness of his humanity. Hidden beneath this answer is the implication that his humanity (and therefore his temptation) was not actually just like ours, which is heresy. Before we move forward, we should all be utterly convinced that "he had to be made like his brothers *in every respect*, so that he might become a merciful and faithful high priest... For because he has suffered when tempted, he is able to help those who are being tempted" (Hebrews 2:17-18, my italics).

Others will say that he remained without sin by simply not *obeying* his temptations. In other words, they acknowledge that he experienced all the same sorts of temptations that we feel but that he never *acted out* on these desires. This is certainly true, but his sinlessness is more meaningful than just his outward behavior. The problem with this view is that it reduces sin to mere actions, despite Jesus himself saying explicitly that it is what flows *from the heart* that defiles a person (see Matthew 15:19-20). In the Sermon on the Mount, this is one of Jesus' main teachings. Not only murder is sin, but anger. And not only adultery is sin, but lust. Etc. God judges the heart, so to be perfect according to the law, the heart must be entirely void of evil desires and perfected in love. That is the true meaning of

Jesus' sinlessness — a heart that was perfectly pure, never once defiled by an evil desire.

So then what does it mean that Jesus was tempted? Does not "temptation" imply that evil desires are in the heart? And if so, then how was Jesus not defiled when tempted?

The reason we have struggled so much to understand this is because (as we discussed in Chapter 2) we have wrongly assumed that the source of temptation is the heart/spirit. But this cannot be true, for Jesus' spirit was pure. In him, there was no sin. Nothing ever came from his heart that defiled him. Where, then, was the source of this temptation? His flesh, of course! The Word became *flesh*, and he was not tempted by *his own* desire (or else we could not say there is no sin in him), but by the desires of the body of flesh he was in.

Knowing this, we might then ask, *How is it that Jesus never obeyed these temptations?* It would be wrong to simply say that it is because his heart was pure. It is sort of like saying that he never sinned because he was God. It does not do justice to the reality of his temptations, and it insinuates that there was never any real possibility for him to obey them. I am more and more convinced that the reason Jesus never gave in to temptation is that *he knew who he was.* Yes, he was without sin in his heart, but even more, he lived by faith according to his true identity in/as God. In doing so, he never confused the passions of the flesh as his own, and therefore was never deceived. His pure heart would not have done him much good if he was not aware that he had it. So although the flesh waged war against him, just as it does with us, he was able to properly fight back and win through his faith/knowledge of his identity. The flesh made him suffer, but it never made him sin.

A pure heart does not do you much good if you do not believe that you have it. When the flesh causes you to suffer, coming on strong with its unruly passions that wage war against you, do not believe the lie that you are somehow failing in these moments. God does not judge you according to the flesh, so you should not, either. Do not believe the lie that the temptations and weaknesses of the flesh are a product of your spirit. Instead, fight back with the truth, and be encouraged that even Jesus "learned obedience through what he suffered" (Hebrews 5:8). Read that again and take it to heart. Obedience is learned, and it is learned through suffering.

> "Since therefore Christ suffered in the flesh, arm yourselves with the same way of thinking, for whoever has suffered in the flesh has ceased from sin, so as to live for the rest of the time in the flesh no longer for human passions but for the will of God" (1 Peter 4:1–2).

What an amazing verse! Suffering — as a result of denying the flesh and pursuing righteousness — is the very process that tests us and causes us to grow in faith, learning to rely not on what we see and feel but on God's grace and unchanging word. This kind of suffering is not evidence of sin; rather, it may even be the very evidence that we have ceased from sin.

LOOK IN THE MIRROR

"But be doers of the word, and not hearers only, deceiving yourselves. For if anyone is a hearer of the word and not a doer, he is like a man who looks intently at his natural face in a mirror. For he looks at himself and goes away and at once forgets what he was like. But the one who looks into the perfect law, the law of liberty, and perseveres… he will be blessed in his doing" (James 1:22–25).

At one point or another, while reading this book, you may have had this thought: If we are only to *believe*, then how do we make sense of all the commands in Scripture that tell us specifically what to *do*? In the passage above, we find a wonderful answer.

According to James, to encounter the word of God — by hearing it taught, by reading it in our Bibles, etc. — is like looking at yourself in the mirror (assuming that you have been born again). For example, if God's word says do not lust after women, then you *are not* lustful. If God's word says to forgive and to love your enemies, then you *are* forgiving and a lover of your enemies. If God's word says to seek first the kingdom of God, then you *are not* someone who cares about money, possessions, and other worldly things. If God's word says not to fear, then you *are* a courageous and faithful believer. The dos and don'ts of Scripture are actually ares and aren'ts, pertaining to your true image, which is Christ. Take a minute to apply this personally to your own life. What is one thing about yourself that you feel is most contrary to God's character? Once you have identified it, give thanks to God that it is not actually who you are. Say, for instance, it is anger. You could say something like, "Thank you, God, that you have made me a patient, gentle, and loving person." Or take a command within Scripture and then rejoice that it now describes you. For example, the Bible says, "Trust in the LORD with all your heart, and do not lean on your own understanding" (Proverbs 3:5). So I tell God frequently, *especially* when I do not feel it, "I trust you completely! Thank you for putting Jesus' faith in me!"

I would like to reiterate that this is not merely positive thinking, as if we are creating our own truth. Rather, it is belief in an unseen truth, in what God has already accomplished.

God's commands are no longer just rules to follow or even something you need to strive to become. Rather, the whole law has been written on our hearts (see Jeremiah 31:33, cf. 2 Corinthians 3:3). Whatever God's word commands is a *reflection* of who you truly are. How? Because the Word, himself, if you have "received [him] with meekness" (James 1:21), is your new life and identity. This is why, in the same letter (Romans) where Paul says so emphatically that we are no longer under the law, he also says, "Do we then overthrow the law by this faith? By no means! On the contrary, *we uphold the law*" (Romans 3:31, my italics). We are not *under* the law anymore because now the law is *in us*. Therefore it still has a very important purpose — to tell us who we are.

Notice what else he calls this "word" — "the perfect law, the law of liberty" (James 1:25). Instinctively, there is nothing about the words "perfect" and "law" that sound liberating. But that is because we have always looked at Jesus — the perfect one, the fulfillment of the law — as just a picture on a wall. He has been something entirely outside of us, the image of what we are not and what we should strive to become. Surely, under the law, this is exactly how it is! But under grace, Jesus comes into us, and that *picture* of Jesus becomes a *mirror* showing him as our true reflection.

It is now easier to see what is happening when we are disobedient to God's commands. According to James, it is like walking away from the mirror and forgetting what we are like (James 1:24). Striking, isn't it? He does not say that if we sin, it is because we are still sinners in need of more grace. Nor is it because we do not love God enough. Instead, if we sin, it is because we *forgot* (or did not *believe*) that we are saints in love with God. Sin, therefore, is a product of deception (which he says in v. 22), and righteousness is truth. If we sin, it does not necessarily mean we are unrighteous. It means that we did an unrighteous thing, out of character, because we believed a lie.

This changes the way that we repent, does it not? If the actual fault was due to *unbelief*, then (as I have said many times already) repentance is *belief*. Sin is no longer an accurate reflection of who you are. It is the result of not seeing your true reflection, who is Jesus. This is different for the believer and the unbeliever, to be clear. For the unbeliever, repentance requires a surrendering of one's life to Jesus, that they might die to sin and live to righteousness. But for the believer, repentance is the remembrance of that death that has already occurred and the new life that has been given. For the believer, true repentance does not entail trying to change yourself or praying that God would finally change you. Nor does it entail mulling over your depravity and beating yourself up for it. True repentance is to acknowledge that what you did was based on a lie. It is to turn back around, look into the mirror, see Jesus, and believe. The one who perseveres in this "will be blessed in his doing" (James 1:25).

A FINISHED WORK OR A PROCESS?

Regarding the way I speak about the finished work of Jesus Christ, a common concern some people have is that they hear me claiming that believers are already perfect and sanctification is not a process. Hopefully, you have already seen that this is not what I teach. But in the case that you are still wondering, I will attempt here to remove your concerns.

At the root of the issue is not *whether* there is a process, but rather, *what* is the process. We just need to define it. Thus far in the book, I have not argued against a process, but I have argued that the church's general understanding of the process has been wrong.

Perhaps the easiest way to explain it is to use the language of the "mind" and "heart." *Before* receiving Jesus into one's life, the heart needs renewal, no doubt. For "[t]he heart is deceitful above all things, and desperately sick..." (Jeremiah 17:9). But as we discussed in Chapter 2, and then much more thoroughly in Chapter 3, God has fixed this problem by giving us new, clean, and pure hearts, upon which God has written his law, and in which the Holy Spirit dwells. Therefore, contrary to popular teaching, believers no longer need renewed hearts. They need renewed minds.

Here are four critical verses that speak to this reality[19]:

---

[19] It is worth noting that, in the following verses, the word translated as "self" (Greek: *anthropos*) literally means "man." In my opinion, the word "self" is misleading because it perpetuates the horrible "dueling-selves"

"Do not be conformed to this world, but be transformed by the *renewal of your mind...*" (Romans 12:2, my italics).

"Though our outer self is wasting away, our inner self *is being renewed day by day... as we look not to the things that are seen but to the things that are unseen*" (2 Corinthians 4:16, 18; my italics).

"[P]ut off your old self, which belongs to your former manner of life and is corrupt through deceitful desires, and... *be renewed in the spirit of your minds*, and... put on the new self, created after the likeness of God in true righteousness and holiness" (Ephesians 4:22–24, my italics).

"[Y]ou have put off the old self with its practices and have put on the new self, which is being *renewed in knowledge* after the image of its creator" (Colossians 3:9–10, my italics).

These passages share a consistent message that there is a continual need for renewal in the Christian life. It is clear that the intended readers — ourselves included — are not perfect. Yet there is another consistent message regarding the kind of renewing that needs to occur. Once again, it is not a matter of the heart or the will. Instead, it is a matter of the mind and the way we think. We need to grow in faith

---

theology that I addressed in Chapter 2. More accurately, the "old man" or "outer man" refers to the *body of flesh*, not a person/spirit within the body. This is especially clear within the greater of context of 2 Corinthians 4 and Colossians 2-3.

and knowledge, learning to walk according to a spiritual reality that we cannot yet see fully. In doing so, the Spirit who has already sanctified our hearts will increasingly sanctify our thoughts and actions, manifesting the righteousness of God, which has been there all along.

To put it simply, the more clearly we "see" — with the eyes of faith — the more we mature into who we truly are. Therefore the reason we are not yet perfect, despite having clean hearts, is because we cannot see perfectly into this spiritual reality. In other words, we lack revelation.

One of my favorite verses that alludes to this fact is this:

> "Beloved, we are God's children now, and what we will be has not yet appeared; but we know that when he appears we shall be like him, *because we shall see him as he is*" (1 John 3:2, my italics).

Notice the reason that we will be like Jesus — *because we shall see him as he is.* It sounds to me like John is saying that, upon seeing Jesus, we will spontaneously combust into our new and glorified forms! How awesome! But even more interesting to me is the insinuation that the only thing keeping us from being just like Jesus now is that we do not yet see him clearly. My takeaway: whatever degree of his glory we currently behold is the degree of his glory that we are capable of sharing (see 2 Corinthians 3:18).

Here is yet another example of the same profound biblical truth:

> "For we know in part and we prophesy in part, but when the perfect comes, the partial will pass away...

For now *we see in a mirror dimly*, but then face to face. Now I know in part; then I shall know fully, even as I have been fully known" (1 Corinthians 13:9–10, 12; my italics).

Remember the mirror-analogy that we covered in the last section? In the verse above, Paul employs the same analogy[20]. One day we will see Jesus *face to face*, lacking no knowledge, and we will thereby be made perfect. But in the meantime, we see him in the mirror, by faith, and the reflection is comparatively dim. Thus, we still press onward to perfection — not by striving to look more like Jesus, but by striving to see how we already do.

I also believe it is helpful to make a distinction between *perfection* and *purity*. The Greek word that is most often translated as "perfect" in the Bible is *teleios*. The root of this word is *telos*, which means "end." Therefore, *teleios* means something like "mature," "adult," "finished," or "complete," indicating that an end goal has been reached. "Pure," on the other hand, means something like "unadulterated" or "undefiled." Therefore, a pure heart describes a heart with unstained innocence or the absence of evil desire.

Using these definitions, we might describe an infant as being *pure*, but never as *perfect*. Biblically speaking, perfection is the opposite of infancy or immaturity, not impurity. Therefore, in our own spiritual infancy, we can just as rightly claim to have pure hearts without claiming to be perfect. Despite having an entirely clean conscience, we still need to grow into our new identity by developing the

---

[20] I am inclined to think this was a widely used teaching in the early Church

mind, without which we remain vulnerable to deception and error, just as a small child.

It is worth noting that even Jesus was *made* "perfect through suffering" (Hebrews 2:10; see also Hebrews 5:8-9), yet his heart was pure his entire life. He was holy and righteous in all his affections and desires. Or in other words, he was without sin. Yet he still had to grow — through the testing of his faith — before reaching perfection, which describes a fully mature human. If this was true for Christ, then why not also for the Christian? While purity describes a heart untainted by sin, perfection describes the full-grown product of someone with a pure heart.

Think of it this way. A tomato plant is a tomato plant, whether it has born fruit yet or not. From the moment the seed is planted and begins to grow, it is a *pure* tomato plant, in that its nature, its identity, does not vary one bit. Even when the plant is just a couple inches above the ground, months away from bearing any fruit at all, it is still as much a tomato plant as it was on its first day of life and as it will be on the last. But it does not become mature or perfect until it is fully grown and bears its best fruit.

So it is with the Christian life. From the moment of belief and conception, Christ is our life, our nature, our full identity — *whether or not* we have begun to bear fruit. If we are abiding in Christ, then there is no sin in our hearts. If there is sin in our hearts, then we are not abiding in Christ, nor abiding in truth. And in this case, we are not able to bear any good fruit. As Jesus said himself, "A healthy tree cannot bear bad fruit, nor can a diseased tree bear good fruit" (Matthew 7:17–18). We cannot bear the fruit of righteousness if we are not already righteous in a real sense. Therefore, "let no one deceive you. Whoever practices righteousness is righteous, as [Jesus] is righteous" (1 John 3:7). We cannot obey God if we have not actually become obedient from the heart. "But thanks be to God, that you who were once slaves of sin have become obedient from the heart..." (Romans 6:17). The work is finished in this sense. Now we must learn to walk by faith in the finished work, and as a result, we will progressively mature into the full-grown image of Christ.

LIKE CHRIST VS. IN CHRIST

A Bible word search will reveal to you that the phrases "in Christ," "in him," "in the Lord," etc. (those which refer to Jesus) appear over 200 times in the New Testament. Guess how many times "like Christ" appears. Zero. What about "like him" (in reference to Jesus)? Twice — Philippians 3:10 and 1 John 3:2. Even if you use a translation that is less literal, you will not find "like Christ" more than five times, and none of them are an accurate translation of the Greek.

Here is the point that I am trying to make. "In Christ" is the most common biblical description of the state of a Christian, yet to most, it has become a practically meaningless expression. We read past it without a thought, assuming it to be merely flowery language. On the other hand, "like Christ" is hardly biblical at all, and yet it has become to many the highest goal of the Christian life. This may seem like nothing, but it makes all the difference in the world as to how we understand our righteousness.

The gospel of "Christ-likeness" is deceptively works-based if we fail to recognize that our *likeness* is purely the product of our *oneness*. In other words, we are never to think of ourselves as *like him* apart from our identity *in him*. The life of Christ is not a mere *example* that we are supposed to follow. If it is, then we are most utterly under the law, and we have nothing but self-righteousness. Instead, Christ is a *person* with whom we have been joined. The only light we shine is Light himself. From the beginning to the end of the Christian life — from infancy to maturity — it is *Christ's* righteousness that is manifest in us. This is why Paul speaks of "not having *a righteousness of my own* that comes from the law, but that which comes through faith in Christ, the righteousness from God that depends on faith" (Philippians 3:9, my italics). Sanctification is not so much the process of Jesus making us more like himself; it is Jesus himself being more and more manifest in us, which is the fruit of our ever-increasing faith. "[N]ow the *righteousness of God* has been manifested apart from the law... the *righteousness of God* through faith in Jesus Christ for all who believe" (Romans 3:21-22, my italics).

We do not fix our eyes on ourselves, claiming to be perfect. We fix our eyes on Jesus, our new life, and we dare to believe that "It is no longer I who live, but Christ who lives in me" (Galatians 2:20). Anything apart from him is not truly who we are. Do not let anyone convince you — Satan or otherwise — that this is a blasphemous thought. It is in your Bible, and it is time to start believing it. It takes the utmost humility to believe and receive this grace, for it allows no room whatsoever for even a trace of self-righteousness. We do not claim to *be* Jesus, nor even to be *like* Jesus. Rather, we claim to be *in Jesus*, and he in us. For "Christ is all, and in all" (Colossians 3:11). It truly is *all* by grace through faith.

Chapter 10

THE EVIDENCE AND PURPOSE OF GENUINE FAITH

Some still may mistake my perspective on the gospel as providing false comfort to those "believers" who willfully continue in sin. They hear me proclaiming that it is *all through faith*, and they equate my message with cheap grace. They assume that I am abdicating the believer of the responsibility to respond to the gospel with repentance, obedience, denial of self, etc. In this case, we have made it full circle back to Romans 6, which we discussed in Chapters 1 and 6 of this book. There, we see that many of the early Christians believed the very same thing about Paul's teachings, but this was only because they did not understand grace.

THE GOSPEL IS A SWORD

The gospel, in its purest form, and grace in its fullest sense, is like a sword that divides. It confronts everyone who hears it with one of two options. (1) Believe, die to oneself, and live through Jesus, or (2) Disbelieve, live for oneself, and die eternally. (1) Believe, die to sin, and live to righteousness, or (2) Disbelieve, live in sin, and die by the law. There are no alternatives and nothing in between. Therefore, the enigma that we addressed in the first chapter exists no more. If we are preaching the full extent of grace and faith, then we need not worry about it minimizing the importance of obedience or enabling believers to continue on in sin. All who truly believe it will be utterly bound to righteousness. That is just how this grace works.

The reason that this has not been evident in our Church, I think, is that the gospel has not been preached in its entirety. The problem is not that believers need to die more to their sin. It is that they have already died to sin, and they do not know it, so they cannot help but continue living in it (see Romans 6:2). It is not that they lack love for God, but that they have no idea how much they love God (see Romans 5:5). It is not that they desire to walk according to the flesh, but that they still identify with the flesh, believing that its desires are their own (see Romans 8:9, cf. Galatians 5:17). The truth sets us free, and they have not heard the whole truth. They have not heard of their identity in Christ, let alone been taught how to walk in it day by day. So despite their clean, repentant hearts and genuine faith in Jesus, they remain in bondage to their sin, much like unbelievers. But I have seen firsthand how quickly this changes when Christians begin to see themselves clearly through Christ and his finished work.

What our Church needs, perhaps more than anything else, at this vital moment in history is to restore these foundational truths of the gospel. I have written this book for that very purpose, with confidence that the Truth radically transforms all who receive it. But the truth is dangerous in this sense, as well — in that once you learn it, there is no going back. It either delivers you from sin or condemns you in your sin; there is no cozy place in between. It either propels you forward or leaves you behind; you cannot keep with it and stay where you are. It calls for perseverance because it always calls you deeper. To believe it *is* to obey it, and to disobey it *is* to disbelieve it (see John 3:36). When the truth is made fully known, there is no saving faith that keeps the believer lukewarm.

Therefore, before we finish, I must issue a stern warning to those who have no plans to move forward in the light. If you readily receive the forgiveness of sins yet knowingly deny the rest of the grace that delivers you from your sin, there is no salvation for you. Do not be deceived. Genuine faith is *always* accompanied by the intent to be holy.

> For if we go on sinning deliberately *after receiving the knowledge of the truth*, there no longer remains a sacrifice for sins, but a fearful expectation of judgment... Anyone who has set aside the law of Moses dies without mercy on the evidence of two or three witnesses. How much worse punishment, do you think, will be deserved by the one who has trampled underfoot the Son of God, and has profaned the blood of the covenant by which he was sanctified, and has outraged the Spirit of grace? (Hebrews 10:26–29, my italics).

EVEN THE DEMONS BELIEVE

As a preacher at my local church, I was often passionate and vocal about our need to flee from sin and seek to live in holiness. I would frequently share my struggles with sin, as well as my insatiable desire to be free from it. I was young, and this added to the common perception that I was just overzealous and naive. Apparently, the seasoned folk knew better than to get riled up over sin, so it never failed that after each of these sermons, I would hear things like, "Don't be so hard on yourself. Why are you so serious? Nobody's perfect. You just need to learn to rest in God's goodness." But let me ask an important question. Cannot a zeal for holiness coexist with a deep knowledge of God's mercy? Should not the thought of continuing in sin be the most repugnant thing on earth to those of us who have been saved from it? If not, I do not know what Bible you are reading. "Like a dog that returns to his vomit is a fool who repeats his folly" (Proverbs 26:11). I know God's goodness. I know his love. And it is this knowledge that stirs within me a deep hatred for sin and an intense desire to press on toward the goal that he set before me. The flame of love that began in me in my justification is the exact same flame that makes me burn for sanctification. Smother one, and you will smother the other.

It is a tragedy that Christians cannot see these kinds of statements for what they really are — a veiled attempt to find comfort in one's sin. I am not saying it is always intentional; it may often be subconscious. Perhaps it is just a way of handling the pain of disappointment, having tried years to be free of sin, and never finding the way. And to be totally fair, I was not preaching the gospel as I now know it.

I was preaching the "try harder" gospel, as I did not yet know the way in which grace and faith alone could bring about holiness. Be that as it may, having learned the way of righteousness, there is no excuse now to remain in this clouded state. "[A]fter receiving the knowledge of the truth" (Hebrews 10:26), there is no shrinking back (see Hebrews 10:38-39).

> "'[B]ut my righteous one shall live by faith, and if he shrinks back, my soul has no pleasure in him.' But we are not of those who shrink back and are destroyed, but of those who have faith and preserve their souls" (Hebrews 10:38–39).

So I say this with compassion, but also with loving conviction. When Christians cannot bear to be exhorted or admonished; when they cannot hear of the glorious perfection to which we were all called in Jesus; when they cannot believe that a brother who is faithfully straining forward is doing so with peace in his soul; it is an obvious sign that they have not yet received or understood God's grace. For if they had, there would be no qualms about pursuing this holiness, and they would seek it themselves with unrelenting fervor.

Why do some feel the need to exalt God's forgiveness at the expense of our high calling to holiness? Perhaps it is because they have not yet come to terms with how far they have fallen short. They agree that we are no longer condemned, but they have found this freedom, not really in the precious blood of Jesus and the high cost he paid, but in the "acceptable" decency of their own life and the little debt they owe. In other words, they have reasoned that their "effort" is "good enough" according to God's "mercy," but they have mistaken God's mercy to mean that he has lowered his standards for mere humans. "Only Jesus was perfect" means to them that only Jesus was called to perfection, so we no longer need to bother trying to attain it. Do you see what has happened? They have found false comfort in a low bar, and it is made clear by the fact that when you raise the bar to perfection, they immediately feel condemned. Make Jesus the standard, and they feel the crippling pressure to perform and the resulting weight of unworthiness that is the product of their works-righteousness mindset, which they never fully left behind.

This whole mindset, which embraces mottos like, "I'm just a sinner saved by grace" and "No one is perfect," pervades the Western Church today. While these statements may hold some truth, the mindset which usually breeds them is a complete misrepresentation of the gospel. It purports to be the most humble and God-honoring posture a soul can have, when in reality, it is little more than apathetic and disrespectful. It is a misguided pendulum swing away from the *grueling* form of works-based righteousness (where the bar is something close to perfection) and into a much *easier* form of works-based righteousness (where the bar is nowhere near perfection). But it never transfers us out of works-righteousness and into the realm of faith and grace; therefore, it undermines the work of Jesus Christ.

They can call it "faith" if they like, but it is only faith in the fact that they are "doing their best" and that their best is "good enough" to be confident God will save them. In other words, they have come close enough to their subjective understanding of "good," "decent," and "moral" that they cannot imagine how God would deem *them* undeserving of Jesus' blood. *But didn't Jesus die for all?* they will say. Yes, "that those who live might no longer live for themselves, but for him who for their sake died…" (2 Corinthians 5:15).

They may say they believe in God's "grace," but to them, his grace is merely an excuse to be happy remaining as they are while they wait for heaven to come. Let us make no mistake, this is neither the faith nor the grace that saves. Rather, it is the very thing that non-believing persons call hypocrisy. For then, why should all, who live similar and decent lives, not in the same way be saved? Are not all these "decent" people just as deserving? The rest of the world sees it; now it is time the Church does, too.

Surely, some will object to my findings, asserting on behalf of all those who have less assurance in their salvation that we need only to *believe* in Jesus to be saved. But in James, we find the clearest proof that belief alone does not accurately describe the whole meaning of faith. For "even the demons believe — and they shudder" (James 2:19). Yet how many bearing the name of "Christian" continue in love with the current world, living for themselves and pursuing the passions of the flesh, all the while resting in the false security of their "belief" and a heaven they will never see? Their lives are a broken commandment — "You shall not take the name of the LORD your God in vain" (Exodus 20:7). The name of Christ is emptied of its glory in these so-called "Christians." Yet they continue to be told that their "faith" will save them. Are we not doing them (and everyone else) a great disservice by giving them the assurance they should not have?

Hear me now. If over time, their lives are not bearing the fruit of righteousness, then they either (a) do not understand what it means to have been born again or (b) have not actually been born again. If the former is true, then good shepherding and teaching is needed. If the latter is true, then we should have no fellowship with them since our fellowship is only with those walk in the light (see 1 John 1:7). Cast them out of our midst, that they might see themselves as they are and genuinely repent.

> "[Y]ou are to deliver this man to Satan for the destruction of the flesh, so that his spirit may be saved in the day of the Lord" (1 Corinthians 5:5).

Some will insist that I should not speak this way about the Bride of Christ. But rest assured, nominal believers (those who take his name, but not his cross) are no more His Bride than the believing demons to which James refers. In fact, you might even say the demons are *better* believers. At least the demons tremble at the name of Jesus, and rightfully so! For they see themselves as they truly are, and Jesus as he truly is, in all his glory and righteousness. Thus, we must come to no other conclusion than this. Belief alone makes no one a Christian. This is why Christ said, "*Repent* and believe" (Mark 1:15); "And whoever does not take up his cross and follow me is not worthy of me" (Matthew 10:38; c.f. Matthew 16:24); and "Whoever would save his life will lose it, but whoever loses his life for my sake will find it" (Matthew 16:25; c.f. Matthew 10:39; Mark 8:35; Luke 9:24 and 17:33; John 12:25). The believer must leave the old life behind and follow. This is not *in addition* to faith; it is *the substance* of faith — that we have died to ourselves, and we live unto him.

If anyone is wounded by these words, please let them recognize what has wounded them. It is the "sword of the Spirit, which is the word of God" (Ephesians 6:17).

> "For the word of God is living and active, sharper than any two-edged sword, piercing to the division of soul and of spirit, of joints and of marrow, and discerning the thoughts and intentions of the heart. And no creature is hidden from his sight, but all are naked and exposed to the eyes of him to whom we must give account" (Hebrews 4:12-13).

Yet God is patient and kind, rich in mercy, slow to anger, and abounding in steadfast love. If you give your life to Jesus Christ, he will give you his own. He will come into you, as well as bring you to himself, and he will make you pure and blameless and righteous as he is. Let the amazing grace of God lead you to repentance, to faith in Jesus Christ, and onward to glory. Put off the old, put on the new, and never look back.

A FINAL EXHORTATION TO LOVE AND PRAY

I have shared the truths in this book with many fellow believers now, and in all my excitement for them to see and experience the power of the gospel, there are two critically important things that I am continually having to learn. The first is that many do not receive it immediately, but if I am faithful in praying for them and continuing the conversation, then they eventually will.

It should not really be surprising that the gospel is met with some resistance, even when it comes to sharing with

Christians. To put it simply, it is almost *too* incredible that God would do what he has done, and a lot of contemporary theology seems to oppose it. I did not believe all this immediately, either. It took quite a bit of time for me to process through everything and come to a place of confident belief. For instance, I remember praying for weeks about whether or not my heart was actually new and pure, like God's word appeared to be telling me. Probably hundreds of times, I asked, "God, can this really be true? Am I crazy? You have to show me!" First, he would confirm it with Scripture, and then in one way or another, he would confirm it in my soul. But this process of growing in faith and understanding is just that — a process. It almost always takes time.

My point here is that, whether you are a pastor leading your congregation or just a friend sharing with another friend, do not expect them to get it right away. That would be unrealistic and unfair. Pray, assume the best, and do not get discouraged. The ministry of the word is a labor of love, and "[l]ove bears all things, believes all things, hopes all things, endures all things" (1 Corinthians 13:7). Continue looking and praying for opportunities to minister the word. Then patiently intercede on their behalf, asking that God opens the eyes of their hearts, and believing that he will. I see him do it all the time.

The second thing I have learned is that all this talk about *faith* and *truth*, while highly necessary, can have a way of overshadowing something even greater — *love*. You may now find, after reading this book, that you have many wonderful truths to start believing in, walking in, and even sharing with others. That is good. But be sure of this — there is no truth greater than that of God's love for you, as well as the love (for him) that he has put within you. If you do not learn to joyfully rest in him and his love — which is the primary purpose of your faith, anyway — then no matter how much truth you know and believe, the amazing gospel life will elude you. The first and most important place to put your faith into practice is by learning to abide in God.

While we certainly must learn to walk by faith, let us never forget that faith is only the *means*, not the end. It is the means to God. It is the means to grace. It is the means to obedience. It is the means to eternal life. But all these — God, grace, obedience, eternal life, etc. — could be very well described as *love*. Love is the substance of Christian existence, without which our faith is empty and meaningless (see 1 Corinthians 13:2-3). If faith is the pen, then love is the ink. "For in Christ Jesus neither circumcision nor uncircumcision counts for anything, but only *faith working through love*" (Galatians 5:6, my italics).

It is imperative that we know who we are in Christ. That is my main reason for writing this book. But this new understanding of our *identity* in Jesus should never replace our *relationship* with Jesus himself. Rather, its purpose is to define and support the relationship. For example, how wonderful it is to know that we are clean, but this knowledge alone will never satisfy the soul. God has done this work and given us this knowledge *so that* we could be perfectly intimate with him. And only here is our soul satisfied. Christ is our *life*, yes. Yet, even more, he is our *lover*.

In practice, it is unfortunately quite easy for this identity message to be warped into something like self-affirming babble, where we go throughout our day just proclaiming truth over ourselves: *I am strong. I am patient. I am joyful. I am loving. Etc.* The problem with this kind of thinking is that it causes us to put all the focus on ourselves. In this way, it actually works *against* love since love draws our attention away from ourselves. The gospel should always draw our attention toward Jesus so that every attempt to believe in the truth brings us nearer to him in prayer, to a place of love and rest. Real gospel-talk sounds more like this: *Jesus, you are strong. You are patient. You are joyful. You are Loving. And because we are one, this is who I am, too! Thank you for giving me your Spirit and making me new. Thank you that I am in you and you in me right now. What a wonderful mystery that I ask you to help me see more fully! You are perfect, Jesus. I worship you, and I love you with my whole heart.* This is just one example, but hopefully, you can see the difference between the two.

One of the most common pitfalls when it comes to walking by faith is that the *truth* becomes a lifeless statement of facts rather than the living God inside of you. You can "walk in truth" all day and every day, but until you capitalize that 't' in Truth, it will be burdensome and powerless to you. Rather than free you, you may even find that it turns and condemns you as you continually fail to live up to its standard. This is just what happens when we talk to ourselves and not to God. Believing the truth is not merely believing the right facts. It is abiding in the person of Jesus, who himself is Truth (see John 14:6). If you ever realize that you are caught up speaking to yourself — especially as it pertains to matters of faith — just stop and talk to God instead. Even better, when you are done talking, allow space to listen. Then wait on his response, trusting that it will come (see James 1:5-8), all the while striving to rest in him. This is when faith really begins to blossom.

Among those who know the truth, I believe there are essentially two kinds of Christians. There are those who pray and those who do not. There are those who rest in God and those who work for God. There are those whose faith depends on God and his word, and there are those whose faith depends on what someone else says about God and his word. There are those who take things before the Lord and say, "Teach me." And there those who rely on their own understanding. There are those who, in the midst of trials, talk to God, and seek his wisdom. And there are those who talk to themselves and try to remember the "right answer." There are those who are driven by love, and there are those who are driven by knowledge. Regarding these two categories of Christians, the former grow tremendously righteous, and the latter grow terribly frustrated. The former become increasingly alive; the latter, increasingly dead. The former bear the fruit of God, and the latter bears the fruit of man.

After all that you have learned, do not be deceived. With whatever amount of faith you currently have, come to Jesus and know him. *This* is eternal life (see John 5:39; 17:3).

END OF BOOK

Thanks for reading. I'd love to hear from you. Visit jakehotchkiss.com, and let me know how this book has helped you. I need your input to make the next version of this book and my future books even better.

If you would like to help me spread the word about the amazing power of the gospel, please leave this book a helpful review on Amazon, and share with your friends.

Sincerely,
Jake Hotchkiss

Made in the USA
Monee, IL
04 August 2024

62672563R00111

The Little Red Light

Fr. Benjamin A. Garcia

Dedication

To my parents, who from
childhood took me to Church.

———

Acknowledgments

My Catechists and Paula Snyder,
who pushed me to finish this
book and publish it.

About The Author

Fr. Ben is a priest of the Archdiocese of Washington. Originally from Chile, Fr. Ben loves to write, play the cello, pray, hike, and the outdoors. Since an early age, he was fascinated by what was happening in front of the Church, but as part of a large family, they always sat in the back. Fr. Ben says, "The red light was for me something important. It meant God was there." That is how this story came to life.

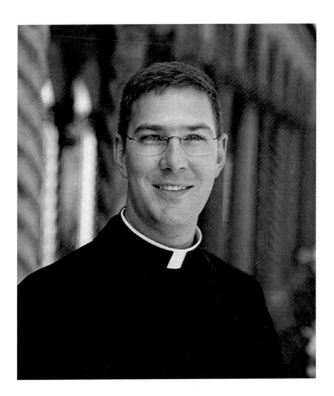

About the Illustrator

Marina is a graphic designer and illustrator based in Central Texas specializing in organic illustration and branding. She was always artistic growing up, and realized she wanted to pursue graphic design in college when she started to become enamored with beautiful packaging designs while browsing the grocery isles during her shopping trips. Now, with over 10 years of experience in the design industry, she continues to experiment and develop her skills with passion and expertise. Marina is a full-time freelance designer and takes on various types of design and illustration projects, but especially enjoys diving into illustration projects such as this one to continue to push her abilities.

Her passions include the outdoors, coffee, loving on her animals, Mexican food, and all things regarding Texas culture.

This is the story of how Fr. Ben found
a Light that conquered his heart...

Since he was a child, Fr. Ben was fond of the light. This is the story that he remembered on the day he was going to be ordained (to become a priest), of how since he opened his eyes to light and life, he found one light that captured his heart and gave him life.

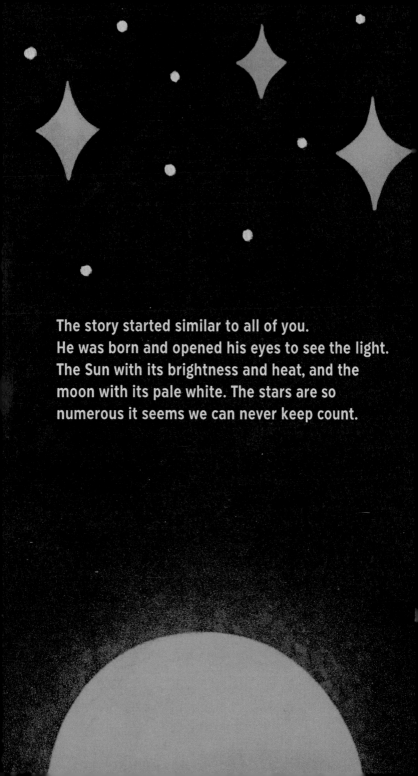

The story started similar to all of you.
He was born and opened his eyes to see the light.
The Sun with its brightness and heat, and the
moon with its pale white. The stars are so
numerous it seems we can never keep count.

As he grew up, he saw many lights. Some made you stop, and some made you move. But there was none like the Sun.

There was one light that he liked as a child. It stood in his room and had been used by his siblings with great delight. Mom and Dad put it to make him always feel right. He was sometimes afraid of the dark, but this light helped him sleep and be at peace through the night.

However, one little light stood more mysterious and wonderful than others he had seen.

In Church, near the altar, he saw this little red light that always shined. It was hard to see when other lights were on, but it always stood still and kept its flame on. This was no ordinary light, for it pointed to Someone who was much more; that little red light pointed to the presence of Christ.

He learned that the red light near the beautiful, mysterious box meant that God was present there, so Big and so Small, to protect him and guide him in all his desires. People would kneel, some with tears and others with joy, but all would find in THIS light the hope they desired and the joy of their lives.

Like the light in the bedroom that kept him safe at night, this little red light that pointed to Christ gave people and him the hope that everything would be all right.

So, every time little Ben went to Mass, he was sure he was okay because God was with him. As long as the red light was on, he knew he was going to be alright, for God was there. It wasn't to the little red light he spoke but to Christ, whom he knew was there. The little red light pointed to the Real presence of Christ the Lord.

For Christ said: "I am the Light," so there is no need for other lights to keep you safe, and every day, remember that it will be all right. On the day he was going to be ordained, Fr. Ben knelt in front of the red light that from childhood had captivated his heart.

The light of Christ the Lord, now, was going to be his guiding force. He was now going to be in charge of guiding people so that they also would know who was the true light, so that even at night or when it gets dark, remember that the little red light is always alight, to tell us, you and me, that Christ never changes and is always there, to help and guide us to be good and safe

For His love for us never changes. We can be sure of that. So, whenever you are afraid or need help, remember the red light that is always on, and believe He is with you now. Visit Him often and learn to talk to Him, who is the light that led Fr. Ben to trust that in all he did, he would be alright.

I invite you then to try and talk to Him. Tell Him your fears, your joys, and your dreams, and you will find in Him the great friend that is always near. No matter what you say to Him, He will never leave you, for He cares for you and me and is ready to give you all you need for your happiness and life.

Made in United States
North Haven, CT
30 November 2024

61284679R00022